Jeff Mills Track 1 Spider Formation (Jeff Mills / courtesy © AXIS)

Rythim Is Rhythim Track 2 Icon (Derrick May / courtesy © Transmat Music)

Robert Hood Track 3 Kick Dirt (Robert Hood / courtsey © M-Plant)

Plastikman Track 4 Plastique (Richie Hawtin / courtesy © Plus 8 Records)

Sven Väth Track 5 Design Music (Sven Väth, Roman Flügel, Jörn E. Wuttke / courtesy © BMG Ufa)

WestBam Track 6 Beatbox Rocker (WestBam / courtesy © Low Spirit Music/BMG)

Der Zyklus Track 7 Die Dämmerung von Nanotech (Rudolf Klorzeiger / courtesy © Gigolo/GEMA)

Dave Clarke Track 8 The Compass (Dave Clarke / courtesy © Skint Records)

Green Velvet Track 9 Sleepwalking (Curtis A. Jones / courtesy © Music Man Records/Cajual Music)

Luke Slater Track 10 Filter 2 (Luke Slater / courtesy © Mute Records)

Cari Lekebusch Track 11 Yash Cosmic Eggbasket (Cari Lekebusch / courtesy © Lekebusch Musik)

Adam Beyer Track 12 Truesoul (Adam Beyer / courtesy © Truesoul)

Miss Kittin and the Hacker Track 13 Stock Exchange (Michel Amato & Caroline Hervé / courtesy © Gigolo Records)

Ellen Allien Track 14 Erdbeermund (Ellen Allien / courtesy © BPitch Control)

Der Dritte Raum Track 15 Wellenbad (Andreas Krüger / courtesy © Moonquake Music/Virgin)

Thomas Schuhmacher feat. Kaori Track 16 Good Life (K. Saunderson / courtesy © Drive On Music)

Slam Track 17 Lifetimes (Stuart McMillan, Orde Meikle, Tyrone Power / courtesy © Soma Music)

Miss Djax Track 18 Killer Train (Saskia Slegers / courtesy © Djax Records)

Art Center College of Design
Library
1700 Lida Street
Pasadena-CA 91103

D0793659

CENTER COLLEGE OF DESIGN

3 3220 00251 9598

PLEASE CHECK FOR AUDIO CDs +FRONT IN BACK
BEFORE AND AFTER EACH CIRCULATION.
CD #1 + CD #2

raw music material

Art Center College of Design
Library
1700 Lida Street
Pasadena-CA 91103

walter huegli (ed.) in collaboration with martin jaeggi

786.7
R257
2002

Discard

R aw M u si c M at eria l
electronic   music djs   today   photographs by arsène saheurs

Art Center College of Design
Library
1700 Lida Street
Pasadena-CA 91103

scalo   zurich − berlin − new york

Art Center College of Design
Library
1700 Lida Street
Pasadena-CA 91103

why this book? Dear reader

Raw Music Material should open a window into the world of Zurich's *Rohstofflager* club over the past five years.

The initial concept was merely to create a photo archive. All the djs playing at *Rohstofflager* were to be photographed in the same place and from the same perspective, using a wide-angle lens. The first series was shot in the legendary *Steinfels* soap factory's 100-year old warehouse for raw materials. After the club relocated, the djs were photographed at the new location in the former *Accu Battery* factory.

After a while, it became clear that the photos represented much more than just "archive material." They tell the story of the *Rohstofflager* and illuminate, at the same time, a key moment in the development of electronic music. The idea for *Raw Music Material* was born. We expanded the initial concept and started to compile and edit texts and to collect tracks. The book should become a compendium of images, sounds, and voices.

where to go from here? Long considered a boring sidetrack, Zurich has become a stronghold for electronic music in recent

years—not least as a result of the platform created at *Rohstofflager*. It is now absolutely urgent to take new steps to keep up the innovative potential of electronic music. This demanding order has been fulfilled, to some extent, by the new *Tonimolkerei Lounge Club* and the *Electronic Music Radio*, which has opened new perspectives for us. While we focused exclusively on dj music in the past, new roads might lead us to a futuristic blend between light and serious music, and ultimately, to an interface between club culture, new media, and the fine arts. We look forward to this challenge with excitement.

Walter Huegli, June 2002

P.S.: What are your thoughts about the future of club culture, the possible convergences of new media, art, and electronic music? If you have any thoughts, ideas, or experiences, I would appreciate if you would mail them to me: huegli@rawmusicmaterial.com

Library
106 png Sur

Art Center College of Design
Library
1700 Lida Street
Pasadena-CA 91103

J e ff M i l ls

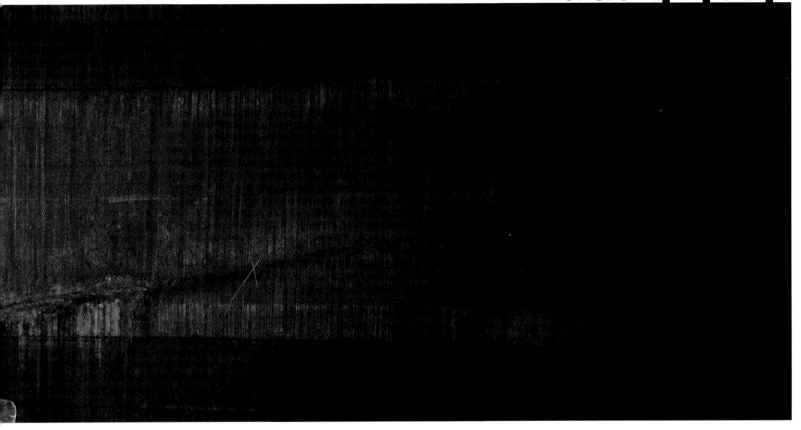

When I started to make music in the summer of '81, it was mainly to support a radio show that I was doing. We were playing music we called "progressive" at the time. It was stuff like Italo remix, *Kraftwerk*, some hip-hop. House music was regarded as shit in Detroit, and we (*Final Cut*, my first band) were going to make an industrial album. But I didn't want to make an album and leave out what I thought was hot. It was all basically an experiment, because I had never made an album before. I didn't even know how to work the equipment all the way. Back then, there was a lot of competition on the radio and my shows were only 45 minutes long so I had to cram as much into that time as I could. I'd just play the best section of each record and move on to the next, so the show had a lot of impact. Nobody could guess what was coming next, but if they'd turn the dial to another station, they'd miss a whole lot of material. I learned to move between records very quickly. Because I had a radio show, I met a lot of people who were trying to make records, or had made records, and they wanted them to be played on the radio. A friend of mine who used to work at the radio station told me that there were these guys called *Members of the House* and they were trying to make a house record. She told me to go by the studio, listen to what they had and see what I could do. So I went by, and that was the first time I met Mike (Banks, co-founder of *Underground Resistance*). I did a mix of *Share this House*, and we kind of kept in touch from that time on. He split from his partner in *Members of the House*, and I split from *Final Cut*. We talked for a couple of weeks and thought it

9

might be a good idea to fuse the two styles together and see what we came up with. The first track was called *The Theory*. We didn't really know what was happening in Europe. We didn't find out what was going on until maybe the fourth release.

In those weeks, we sat down and talked. We had noticed what Kevin Saunderson, Juan Atkins, and Derrick May had been through. The things that they should have done that they didn't do, and why they were in the position they were in. We thought: if we do it, we should manage ourselves, distribute our own records. So we were kind of forced into it, because we didn't really trust anybody. It was pretty easy. I was just a student; I was studying architecture at the time. The demand was there, and we sold a lot of records. The main difference had to be the attitude. The attitude we had with *Underground Resistance* was a more bold attitude: here it is, hardcore from Detroit, revolution for change, music for those who know. This time we were doing it in the spirit of the science of techno, not the agression, but the science of making future electronic music

At one point, I liked the idea of starting over from the beginning. The whole outfit was in Detroit—we had a building, offices, employees, the t-shirts and all that mess. So I said, "You take all this and most of the money." I took just enough to start a new label. Back in Detroit, we did all the tracks together. In the last phase of *Underground Resistance*, Mike Banks was on tour and I sat in the studio alone once. That's when I did *The Punisher* and *The Seawolf*. Detroit is a depressing city. The feel there is kind of dreamy. After the split, I was in a different city, New York, where I was resident dj at Limelight, and my sound changed. It was a really different vibe. I had to get used to New York. I didn't make music for eight months. After listening to what I was playing and what everyone else was playing, Robert Hood (third member of *Underground Resistance*) and I sat down and we figured out what it was we heard. It was something very minimal, with rhythm, very simple so that everyone could understand it. We had to strip down what we knew. All I had learnt with *Underground Resistance* I had to forget. Forget that way of business, forget that militant attitude. Minmalism allows the listener to project more of their imagination onto whatever it is that they're listening to. It's a very open-ended form. We've still got a long way to go before we run out of territory to explore. I really started off on an understanding that techno music was someone's effort to describe something of the future. It's endless to ideas and possibilities. In my mind, we're just beginning the whole process. That's my motivation. We don't live forever, we die away. I think that it's really very important to take very careful steps as to what we do because it is actually laying the groundwork for producers 30 years from now. I try to use a methodical process in constructing each release or project. The physical appearance of each release is taken quite seriously, as each color, word, or figure must have a significance. It is easier for me to understand the ramification of what I have to do if I understand each element of the subject.

I have to keep the people moving. Sometimes you have to check out the vibe at a certain party within 3 records. It is a lot of trial and error on my side that most people do not see. Some djs have a planned set—I don't. I always try to play a special mix for the night. I like to have a transition in my set. I always play house if I can, mixing it in, so it's more like a party. Too much of one thing quickly becomes stupid and you are giving the people exactly what they want. You are following the people instead of vice versa.

I do what I do because I need to. It seems to be the most provocative means for me to communicate with others. If things go right, I have a great satisfaction that what was just created was productive and people might remember it. It provides me with a better understanding of people so that I can somehow use this information to connect even deeper. Being able to remember, I think, is the most important human response we possess. Being able to compete with all the thousands of advertisements, signs, etc., that every person encounters every day, to have someone remember me (or even my name) is a great feat. I will never forget this.

R o ber t Ho od

I don't know exactly why techno started in Detroit. Maybe it's the combination of despair, crime, corruption, and the collapse of the car industry. This creates a very dense atmosphere in Detroit. But you can't pinpoint and explain it. The whole is somehow quite closed, almost like an ineffable secret society. Detroit was always the city of the American car industry, whereas New York was the center of banking, stock exchange, and politics. That has shaped the atmosphere and the architecture of both cities in very different ways. Detroit is a strange little town. New York, however, is huge and the structure of its population is very mixed, open, and multicultural. So techno fits Detroit and hip-hop New York.

When I was about 14 or 15 years old, there was a station called *WLBS*. Between *WLBS* and Electrifying Mojo (a Detroit radio dj, one of the first to play electronic music from Europe), I got influenced by certain artists: *Gary's Gang*, *Telex*, etc.. All of them formed a kind of prophecy. I thought to myself, "It's only a matter of time before this electronic sound and this funk sound and disco sound are going to fuse together." Shortly after that, I started to hear about Derrick May, Juan Atkins and certain progressive parties, and it just started to evolve from there. There was also an artist by the name of Eddy Grant and he did a kind of reggae electronic stuff. Listening to all this, it made me realize that this was what I wanted to do. I got a drum machine from a pawn shop and just started messing with it. I didn't know nothing about MIDI, nothing about djing. I just knew I wanted to do this music and I knew I could do it.

I hooked up with Mike (Bank) and Jeff (Mills) through a mutual friend called Mike Clarke, aka Agent X. He introduced me to Mike, and at that time I had a demo tape, basically just drum tracks, keyboard tracks, and stuff like that, and I was rapping on it. Mike was impressed by my drum programming, so he invited me to his studio. We started recording some tracks at Jeff Mills' house—that's where they did all the recording at the time. They were just starting *Underground Resistance* and they were doing a track for that particular compilation. It was basically just the two of them. At the time, I was just the *Underground Resistance* gofer. I was doing tracks with them for the compilation, but I started working for them, running errands for them, doing artwork, the t-shirts, the record labels and things like that. I came in on an artistic/business side, just helping them to do some administration for the label. They took their time and just groomed me very slowly so that I would understand what I was doing. It was never like, "Oh, let's rush this artist out." I wouldn't have known what I was doing. You have a group of guys and you record together and run a label together and travel together—so you become like brothers. You live together, but at some point you start to disagree on certain things and you just branch off. Jeff wanted to do *Axis Records* (Mills' label) at the time. After a while me and Mike started not to see eye to eye, so shortly after Jeff left, I had to leave because of the lack of mutual respect.

M-Plant (my Label) was an escape from the rave and gabber sound. I didn't want to do that hard 160 bpm stuff. Nothing against it personally, but I saw the whole techno scene going in that direction. Detroit has to maintain its roots, that is all I was thinking. We are talking soul, reality, just the realness. The music was getting too belligerent, too ravey, too circus-like. You know, lights, lasers, smoke and not the reality, no kind of social commentary. Marvin Gaye, Martin Luther King Jr., we've got to take it that way. I'm not saying you have to do it like Detroit does it. Rotterdam is only speaking from Rotterdam experience, Berlin is speaking from their experience. I want to maintain the Detroit sound. That rave sound at the time was just covering that to me. I was more like, "I have to champion Detroit." Soul, funk, and just rhythm. *M-Plant* is about implanting these little thoughts and dreams in the heads of people so everyone can feel what I feel. Every records is like a little implant. I had to look inside myself and say, "What do you like, what do you want to hear?" What I've always wanted to hear: the basic stripped-down, raw sound. Just drums, bass lines, and funky grooves and just what is essential to make people move. I started to look at it as a science, the art of making people move their butts, speaking to their heart, mind, and soul. It's the *M-Plant* in every person's mind that is speaking through your heart, through your soul and is making you dance in the process. To me, rave was just samples. True techno, the true sound of it, is a science. Techno is music based on information and databanks. Thus, I wouldn't exactly call myself a "musician." I am a dj who also makes records. I think that describes me best.

Techno is part of black music, but it works on a much more universal level than, let's say, blues or jazz. And considerably more than rap. More than any kind of music we know so far, techno is a step in the direction of a truly universal music. When house and techno were born, they were very immediate—no long intros, straight to the point. And that was the really innovative aspect of this music, apart from the fact that it was electronically generated. This minimal and repetitive element, the endless repetition. You hear the record and let yourself go, like in a trance. I think that the best pieces of music work with very minimal means: simple songs, simple lyrics, simple melodies, melodies that you can remember. Another reason for minimalism is that people should have the opportunity to think their own things about it and should be inspired by it. Minimalism really is my way of living. I am not exactly a fan of modern lifestyle. I try to focus on the essential and hardly have any useless things. I have my bed and studio equipment—no fridge, no luxury. Unnecessary things like large-screen TV and video games block creativity.

D erri ck M ay

Juan Atkins and I have known each other since childhood, and basically Juan taught me how to be a dj and our philosophy of music and what we should play and how we should approach people in our dj sets. And that sort of mentality flowed over into my everyday life as far as every aspect of what I saw as normality I considered completely disgusting. After I'd met Juan, I realized that there were so many things that people were not interested in and I couldn't understand why … But people just sort of live their lives according to somebody else's rules and never question it. We've all had family and friends that live like that and we don't criticize them, we try to enlighten them. But if they don't wanna know, they don't wanna know. But I was young and we were rebels. I think that when we first did the music, we wanted to believe that we were intellectual; we always wanted to tap into an intellectual level of the black mind. We wanted to show that black people could do something that was hi-tech, but intellectual at the same time. We wanted to prove that you could do something that was hi-tech that you could dance to, but it didn't have to be all about being onstage and shuckin' and jivin' and what not. That was what we enforced mostly about the music. And we stayed with it. And that's why it's been so hard to this day to get approval for what we've done. Because we still refuse to shuck and jive. We're all about showing the aspect, as if to say that we are the modern-day jazz fusion sort of intellectual style of music.

Detroit's not supposedly one of the so-called forefront leaders of ideas and creativity. So people tend to discount it in the media. They don't really say, "Okay, well, Detroit is the focus of music in America." They'll never let that happen. They'll never say that a city like Detroit, which is going through so much economic strife, which is a city full of illiterates at one point, at one level, is the focal point of electronic music, period. So instead of them saying, "This was the shit, what happened in Detroit; they're on top of it, so many people having a great time … Wow, black young guys getting off doing their electronic/tech/techno music," and all these little young white kids coming from around the world to hear this, they won't let that happen. They will constantly discount it, and they will act like this didn't happen. Only history will tell the truth. It will show that Detroit and what we're doing was the shit. It was a real influence on music around the world. If this happened in New York, everyone responsible would be considered geniuses. But it happened in Detroit, so we get nothing.

I like to stay with the sound that has never really been properly discovered, which is the sound of Detroit. The sound of hi-tech tribalism; it's very spiritual, very bass-oriented, and very drum-oriented, very percussive. The original techno music was very hi-tech with a very percussive feel, so there were lots of strings, lots of sounds to the left, then sounds to the right. But it was extremely, extremely tribal. It feels like you're in some sort of hi-tech village. 80% of all my songs have always started with strings, it's like a mood, a frame of mind. I don't always end up using those strings but that's the way I start and from there I just build. I'm a metronome kind of guy, I make the music to the metronome. Tick. Tick. Tick. Tick. The last thing I do is adding the drums. Too many people use drums as a *pièce-de-resistance* to their music. That's dumb. Drums are an accent. That's it. You should be able to make a track and not even use drums. You should be able to have so much power that you don't need drums.

Black people can't get the opportunity to be artists. They can get a chance to be entertainers all they like but they can't get the chance to be true artists. Especially in a genre that hasn't been totally proven. Record companies want to take their chances with marketable people which happens to be people of their gender, color, or race. Maybe it sounds racist. I don't think it is racist. It's business. You've got black kids in this country who won't come out and dance. They don't want to know about dance music. They're not even interested. Half of them don't even know it exists. It's the same shit all over the world, even in Africa. I have been to South Africa and the black folks don't want to know. Nobody has a black audience except for the r 'n' b and rap crowd. I long for a black audience to hear my music. It hurts me to believe that black people are not down. Because I'm black.

K e v i n   S a u n d e r s o n

Everyone associates me with Detroit, but I was in fact born in Brooklyn in '64 and moved to Detroit at the age of nine. There was a lot of violence, a lot of kids killing each other. At one time, all the whites moved out to the suburbs, but now they all want to move back into town again, so a lot of the minorities are getting moved out. It's very depressing, and there's nothing really positive I can say about the city as far as what's going on and the people who are running things. There was a lot of unemployment, a lot of people on welfare. I think the city puts the people in that bad situation, and a lot of young people coming up don't understand why they're in the situation they're in.

It was while attending Belleville High School that I met Juan Atkins and Derrick May, but it wasn't until I went to Eastern Michigan University, where I studied telecommunications and played football that I diverted my attention to making music. Derrick had been spurred on by Juan, who was putting out what would later become future classics like *Cybotron* and that in turn rubbed off on me. Me and Derrick were very close friends, and Juan and Derrick were close friends, and I met Juan through Derrick. As time went on, we became close friends and I kind of was around them. Juan was heavily influenced by European electronic artists, such as *Kraftwerk*, *Depeche Mode*, and *Human League*, and their sound had a big impact on us. It seemed like music of the future to me. *Kraftwerk* had this really clean, computerized, futuristic sound. Their music had a good groove, but at the same time it was deep and you could sit back and listen to it. They had a good image, too. I think what Detroit did for this whole thing is that we made everything danceable. We made it dj-friendly, ready for the clubs. So we took it to another level. And that level became known as techno. When we started creating, we didn't have much equipment. Everything was minimalist. We had a *Roland MDC-500* Sequencer and just a few different things. But it played a very important part because we didn't start out as musicians. The sequencers helped us, because you can get your idea down and keep repeating your idea. We had a board, we had something that we could record on, and an effects unit, which was minimal, but still, that's maybe about $3'000 or $4'000. Back then, that was a lot of money for a college kid to try to come up with. But it was an easier process than trying to go in and use studio time. For one thing, instead of creating, you're worrying about the time that you have to try to create something. The way we started has played a major part in helping our careers, because otherwise spending a $100 a hour or so, I don't think the vibe would be the same. And it's easy because you can get right up and get right into it, too. It's just a natural process. You maximize all your creativity by using that equipment to the fullest extent. Juan was the one who pointed me in the right direction as far as showing me around my technical equipment is concerned, and the fruit of those early sessions was a track called *Triangle Of Love*. There were plen-

ty of times when I woke up in the middle of the night and I went right into the studio, cause my studio, back in the early days especially, was right in my living room. So I just went right next door and I would get a vibe. Sometimes I would have a dream and I would feel like I had to make a track. And I would go in there and just based on how I felt, I would start creating sounds and just get so deep into it. It's almost like another world and time passes on. Before you know it, you have a creation by experimenting with sounds and changing different sounds and blending stuff together. And obviously there's different tempos, different speeds that help that mood. But it's all about that and knowing how to get it out. If I can't create a sound that I like, I find it very hard to create a song. I get inspired by a good sound. It's like a message to me, it gives me a feeling for a rhythm or a melody. The sound's the most important thing. Usually, I start by trying to program a bass sound, cause that's what the music needs. I'll use any of my keyboards. I sit around for hours trying to program sounds that no one else has come up with before, sounds that are going to have a lot of energy. If you use presets, you just end up sounding like everybody else.

When I dj, I feel like I want to give people music that touches them, that they feel something from the music. I think that's the most important. I try to take it and build, build, build, and build. And to intensify the records that I'm playing in order for the energy level to go up. I have always wanted to add things to other people's music, and I feel that I have a good feeling for what people like to hear.

S v en V äth

The biggest joy for me is to have a record in my hands and to know how to make people happy with it at the right moment. That's why I have so much fun. It's incredibly difficult to always be on top of everything because in every area so much is happening, so many records are being released all the time. I get around 100 promos a week. From everywhere. I am an absolute record junkie. I am still on a mission. I've djed for more than 20 years. The pleasure of partying, of dancing, has amounted to something over the years for me. A philosophy, a way of looking at life, the belief in a cause, and it made me question my life, time and again, "What are you doing? Are you on the right track? What's your message? What are giving and what are you getting?" Over the years, I increasingly feel that I use music as a transmitter for myself to give something to people. A spark of pleasure in life, of tolerance. To be together and to let go together, all the way to the extremes. This mission is still the main thing for me. And the nice thing is that the music and new records always provide me with new tools to repackage the whole thing.

I don't feel like I have to hide and say, "No one should see me when I dj. It's all about the music." Bullshit! People always need someone they can connect to and they can identify with. I always felt that I could bring the music across in a more convincing way by using my personality. Because I give people an honest feeling. The most important thing is to see people standing happily on the dance floor in the end. If weren't a dj, I would probably be an actor or a circus artist. I have always loved to give something to people, a feeling, a smile. It doesn't cost a thing.

The fight for techno culture is over and we have won it. To me, we have arrived at a point where I can say, "OK, we have gotten it through, the baby." Because this culture has a life of its own and will go on anyhow. I am not that important anymore. Our ears are trained. There can't be a lot of new things. Some have a straight bass line, others an electro beat, but the musical influences aren't new anymore. From experimental to ambient to break beat, we're immune. What's left that should move us musically? Audio is done, I'd say. Now the question is, "On what level are we going to get this? What are we going to do with it?" The worst thing today is that everyone's trying have a piece of the cake and get a bargain. Still, I have to say that what I have experienced in Germany in the past ten years is amazing. All the people I got to know that have contributed to techno and have seen to it that this thing has grown and the music and the scene are what they are today. That's why I see a future for this music, in spite of the doubts of the past few years. There's a sense of community, otherwise we wouldn't have such dense and large structures, like magazines, labels, producers, record stores, distributors. Just look at it in Germany today—we are the techno nation of the entire world. What happens in electronic music, what is covered here: from blubbering ambient to all facets of house, to trance, minimalism, trip-hop, vanguard electronica like *Mouse on Mars*, and so on. And there's still a considerable freedom we're enjoying. Just look at what is happening abroad. People sometimes have these ideas about the way things are in the UK or the US, for instance, but that's not the case. This techno thing doesn't exist anywhere in this form. When people abroad talk about music in Germany, they talk about electronic music and nothing else, if anything about classical music from the 18th century.

It's always about making contacts, creating contacts, getting people together, using contacts and passing them on so others can use them. I like to build up a type of creative environment where things can happen. You have to give something back, reinvest, put something in it and give young people a chance.

R ichi e Haw ti n

When I moved to Canada from England, I was like 9 or 10 years old, so it was only years later that I started to get into music on principle. Because once all my friends were getting into music in their early teens, at 11, 12, 13, I wasn't really into it. Everyone was into rock music and *The Rolling Stones.* I don't know if I just wasn't into music, or if I just hadn't heard what I wanted. But I was definitely a lot more detached than I was in the UK, where I was more out-going, just a kid, had tons of friends, knew everyone. I was in a village of a couple of thousand people, then suddenly I was thrown into a very American-ized, weird Canadian culture. The reason my parents took us out of there was, to quote a great *Sex Pistols* song, "There's no future." There really was no future in the late 70s. Grim was the word. My parents thought that the only way we would have future opportunities was to take us somewhere else. It was either Australia or Canada. I think when I did find music and electronic music, it did provide an outlet that I could get into that everyone else wasn't into. I was looking for something different, something a little bit more personal. The other big thing was that my father was always into electronics. He was an electrician. When I was a kid, I always had little gizmos—connecting little wires up to the little radio and things. In the mid-70s, my Dad built a whole com-puter by himself, and he always had hi-tech hi-fis and reel-to-reels. I had my own reel-to-reel recording stuff when I was 7 or 8, recording sounds and stuff

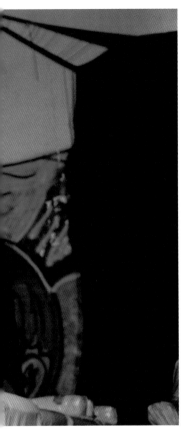

like that. There were always these weird little things that were happening in my house. My father had very eclectic tastes. I can remember him going from things like *Tangerine Dream* to *Fleetwood Mac* and back to *Kraftwerk*. I don't think it had a direct influence on me. It was more like I was being influenced without knowing it at the time. It was only later on when I got into music that I would go back into his collection and recognize albums.

I think techno is the progressive part of electronic music where people are really trying to think outside of the box. Every time you've got some type of success, it usually happens when you are already beyond that point because you're already working on new ideas. Success usually means that people have caught up to what you are thinking. That partly scares me because I don't want to get stuck thinking the way people think and creating music for people at that moment. That way you start working in the past. I also want to have freedom within the thing I am doing. I try to balance it so that I'll have some type of commercial success, some type of accessibility because I like people buying my music. People seem to be a little bit more open-minded when they come to my shows, even if they're people who aren't necessarily train-spotting undergrounders. I want to strike the balance. I don't want to be the knob twiddler in his bedroom, coming up with something that's so crazy that no one's gonna get it, or no one's gonna get it for 20 or 30 years. I want to introduce as many people as possible to a deeper side of electronics, a deeper side of techno, than they regularly get exposed to, and I want to do it in a really quality way, with as little compromise as possible.

People have become more and more interested in electronic music. They have become more aware of the sounds and the structure. As you understand that language, you start to realize that you only need so many words to make a correct sentence. I think we are at the point where people want very precise sentences. Why give someone a whole paragraph when you can say it with a few words? Minimalism to me is just balance, balance within music and balance within life, understanding what exactly is necessary to get your point across. I think with the world we live in, with so much crazy stuff going on, an information overload, the idea of balance and minimalism is more and more attractive every day. I think a lot of what I do is influenced by other art, such as the minimalists of the 50s and 60s. Their art took the chance to express things in a very slight manner, through subtle changes in texture and color. A lot of minimalist art is built from a collection of smaller elements—once a person allows themselves to get into it, the sum of the parts is a lot greater: you realize the space they didn't use. I use these visual ideas and apply them on a sonic level, a lot of it has to do with the spaces between sounds

I want to further explore the interaction between man and machine and the visual and audio world. I also want to explore the way people experience things, the way I can create moments that people will remember. Technology and the way it interacts with all of our senses, that's what interests me. Right now, I have experimented with sound and hearing and perhaps a little bit of sight, so I think there are a number of senses I haven't worked with yet.

As djs we take two pieces of vinyl and we put them together and make a hybrid version. I've used other people's information and I re-evaluated that information and made it relevant to me as an artist and perhaps to this moment in time. As this information moves freely around the internet and around the globe, people will be able to take the stuff and re-evaluate it. The main artist will only make one version, and everybody else will continue to perfect that music. Vinyl is such a linear approach, it's so outdated. When you use digital files, you have full control over how you want to interpret that record, whether it's filtering it, re-mixing it, or taking parts out and re-sequencing it. Things that the artist might not want to happen, but djs are performers and they take these records and re-evaluate them. Using digital files is another way of extending that ability to re-evaluate. It's really time to rethink performance. Dj is an outdated term anyway, period. I think it's going to be common place in the years to come. You know, a computer with a turntable, just samples, digital shit.

W est Ba m

I started djing in '83. As a dj, I noticed that different records could be added up to something of its own. In '85, I made my first record. My music was an outgrowth of my djing. At first, composing was putting together records. Today, I don't put together records so often anymore, but the way of thinking has basically remained the same. I have sampled a lot, but not as a medley or a compilation of quotes. After all, it should not be something that was pieced together, it should be a new form where the single little elements loose any value of their own. I am responsible for what comes about. On the way there, I use traces of others who have created other things. But I would like to see an artist today who claims that his works have been dictated to him from above, as an irregular inspiration of nature. The concept of the genius that Kant cares so much about cannot be used anymore. I believe that everyone assimilates from his environment so that he or others can continue to develop in this environment. The units that I put together were re-processed by other musicians and have been used to create other units. I don't distinguish between samples from groups that I consider good and those from groups that I don't consider good. The samples serve to create a new unit, independent of any ideological judgement on the source material. I don't judge a sound based on the person who created it. The tenet of a rave is to dissolve the works in each other and to destroy them as works. The tracks are totally meaningless in themselves and achieve their temporary meaning only in the mix when the dj uses the material in its context and re-processes it. Only then you can perceive the sound.

For me, the distinction between good and bad music is not based on the boundary between commercially successful music and music without commercial success. A lot of people are always looking for criteria to distinguish good and bad, and some people have agreed to say: this is bad commercial music that was made only to make money, and then there's good underground music, which is about the realization of artistic ideas. Naturally, that's pure black-and-white thinking that doesn't work in most cases, and only works for people who look for particularly simple criteria and who end up contradicting themselves pretty fast. If I like something, I can also play it if it's in the top ten. Generally, the word "commercial" is used to denounce everything that is evil and bad: you say "commercial" and the entire underground eagerly nods its head and says, "It's real shit." In reality, there's considerably less genuinely commercial music than is generally thought, if you take the word seriously and use it for music that was produced with the exclusive or prevalent purpose of making money. "Commercial" always gets confused with "commercially successful," and that's a real difference. When I started, record companies always suggested, "Get a singer, write a song, and do a remix or cover version." And I never really did that. In this sense I have remained true to my stance and I still do what I did in '88 or '89, tracks, that is. Tracks are the opposite of the classical hit, the song. A track is a mixture of sounds, rhythms, shapes, but it's not a song.

I have to admit that the dj pop star was an idea that I liked when I was 18, 19, and I believed that I somehow had to dress up in a funny way. In the course of time, that went out. I came to the conclusion that the good thing about this sort of movement is that the stage in techno is the dance floor and not the dj booth. And when it starts to work differently, it's a wrong direction. In the end, it's not that attractive to look for an entire evening at someone with two decks.

I don't make something completely unequivocal. I am all for multi-functionality. It would be interesting to know in what kind of wave it works, and how it is received. Or why people who never go out and have nothing to do with raving and all it entails buy a 12" to listen to at home. From the perspective of the underground, multi-functionality has to be rejected, but I always considered it interesting. I was pleased when *No More Fucking Rock 'n' Roll* was used at a *Chanel* fashion show and some models were walking around to it, or when an East Berlin TV ballet did a little choreography to *Wetten Dass* before

the wall came down. This is a nightmare to underground aficionados, but I think it's interesting because it's so strange as you never thought that it would be integrated in such a context.

The rave generation went a step further by more or less throwing away the entire super-structure that's been around ever since the hippie generation. I think it's a step in the right direction, towards more honesty, and not a lack thereof in comparison to other youth movements. Johnny Rotten, for instance, said in an interview, "Techno has no meaning," and that it could never measure up to punk. That's crap. Punk, after all, was just pogo dancing, beer spitting, and partying. Punk was shit compared to techno. Punk was just a stupid little fashion created by a sex-shop owner who chased a little band that couldn't play through various venues in England for a year and then they more or less quickly dissolved and that was it, almost. Techno has filled halls over the years on the entire world. Techno has always renewed itself. Techno is the first international music that is not a product of the Anglo-American entertainment industry. Techno is listened to everywhere.

The new thing is probably already around. One characteristic is probably that it won't come from the US. As far as dance culture is concerned, the US are the old world and Europe the new world. Americans carry too much dance tradition around with them. There's no collective musical dance heritage in Europe. That kind of thing really blocks you. Most great and eponymous acts are not committed with the knowledge of something, but much rather in ignorance. This is why dance culture could become so big in Europe.

L a u r e n t G a r n i e r

I've always wanted to be a dj ever since I was 9 or 10 years old. I wanted to be a dj because I wanted to give emotions to people. Basically, I was listening to records and they were giving me something and I wanted to give all of this out. I receive emotions from a lot of types of music and I just want to give all of this out. *Got to be Real* by Sheryl Lynne changed a lot in my life because I discovered disco through that record. I love Donna Summer. It's an acid house track, it's a techno track. Sylvester's *You Make Me Feel.* The break! The way it's done—it's a techno track. Completely techno. Or maybe techno is completely disco?

After compulsory military service, I went to catering school and straight away I got interested in it because they treated us like young adults and not like pieces of shit like schools in France do. I had a wonderful time, met some wonderful people, and my teacher is still a friend of mine. I've never been a chef. I've always been a waiter. I did cooking courses but I was always into the waiting side. I got bored behind my pans, I want to talk to customers. During military service I was djing for three or four hours as well, so I was only getting three or four hours of sleep a night. I was just killing my body. The first house

we heard was was Farley Jackmaster Funk's *Jack Your Body* and all those things. Very quickly after that, Derrick May came to Manchester to dj, and the whole thing began to spiral out of control. The very first one though was that Farley Jackmaster Funk track. It was funky, there were amazing vocals, then after that there was the ba-ba-ba-ba-bom ba-ba-ba-ba-bom, and we were amazed. The most exciting thing about it was that it was fresh—it seemed like we would never get bored of it because it sounded so new. It's changed now, though. There's major music companies that are controlling electronic music, and it's fucking atrocious.

Because my brother was six years older than me, I was very influenced by what my brother was listening to and he was hanging on about the gay scene so disco was very big. I made a tape to give to Paul who was in charge of hiring djs for *Haçienda* (club in Manchester). I mixed fifty tracks in 90 minutes. I knew Paul was gay, so I mixed disco, hi-NRG, salsoul, Philadelphia, and house. Paul called me the day after and said, "Okay you got the job." It was luck because I gave a tape to the right person at the right time. The first time I saw a *Technics 1200* was when I turned up to work at *Haçienda*. I couldn't mix to save my life. That was '87. I've been extremely lucky because I went there at the right time, basically when acid house totally exploded.

I think it's a shame that music has been put in so many compartments—like if you go to a drum 'n' bass club you will hear nothing else. When I started, you had to play a variety of stuff to keep people entertained all night. Unfortunately, I think a lot of clubbers are closing themselves off to a lot of things

and they don't really look around at what's happening around them, which is really sad. Nowadays lot of djs are either techno or house, but they are not really playing both. If I go to a house club and I only hear house, I am bored, and if I go to a techno club and I only hear techno, I am bored. A lot of people today in the techno business have totally forgotten where we come from, and they ghettoize our music and they're killing our music. Strictly playing hard techno, like 90% of the techno djs do. Killing our system and killing the business. Because at the end of the day, these guys don't see any further than these little, hard, energetic loops, like a lot of Scandinavian stuff. We should never forget that the roots of techno have come from other times. Without rock, without *Kraftwerk*, jazz, classical music, funk, electro, which was the beginning of hip hop, without disco, without all of it, we would not have techno music.

Djs are not there to dictate anything, as a lot of djs think. We're just there to give people a good time. It's like a love relationship. When you're having sex with somebody, sometimes it works, sometimes it doesn't, you know? It depends on your mood, what the other person's mood is, what interests them. A crowd is the same. Sometimes you get it, sometimes you don't. The whole thing about what I try to do is to pull the crowd into my own world and once you're there, you can do what you want. But it takes a good two hours to get there. It's a relationship. With every single record you play, you have to put your head up and watch what's happening on the dancefloor because you have to watch the movement. People go blind when they're on the dancefloor.

If there's one part they don't like, they will either leave the dancefloor or they will change their way of dancing. You can see it in their eyes. The biggest thing I do when I dj is to look people in the eyes.

You will not find markets for records tomorrow that you had yesterday—it's not about seeing whether someone gets a number-one hit, then dropping them if they don't. It's all going to happen on the internet eventually. Everything is beginning to change and I find that very exciting. House and techno have progressed so far, and infiltrated so much, that maybe music isn't the next thing. Maybe it's multimedia. I don't know.

C arl Co x

Actually, I was a bouncer before I was a dj—so I kind of came into it from being down at the club and standing on the dance floor all night. I started to realize that I could play better than that, and I found myself behind the decks one day. It was strange being there, it was all the other way round.

Basically, I got started because my family used to have a lot of records, and when I was like eight years old, my mum used to let me play with the records to get me out of the way. I would put these records on, and me, mum, dad, family, and friends would all be dancing about. I can't remember a time without the strains of soul music drifting through our house. With both parents coming from Barbados I was brought up very much in tune with a natural party ethos that went hand in hand with a love of good music. My earliest musical memories are of *Booker T. and the MGs,* Aretha Franklin and, of course, the great Elvis, and I used to hijack my parents collection of 70s soul singles and get the whole family grooving round the lounge. I guess the early signs were there—my passion for music combined with an overwhelming desire to entertain as many people as possible. By the age of ten, I had well and truly caught the bug and was spending every bit of my pocket money on soul and funk records. I got my first pair of decks by the age of 15, and I started to play as many parties as I could, discovering that I could buzz off a crowd while funding my habit at the same time. As the 70s became the 80s, I followed the musical trend from soul to disco to hip-hop, but it wasn't really until I moved to Brighton in '86 that I discovered, along with so many others, the pure thrill of acid house.

What you hear now in clubs is basically a progression of disco music. Cut-ups of disco tunes, which just goes to show that the music which was coming out back then wasn't so bad to begin with. It just took twenty years for people to get their heads around to it. There were two sides to it. There was a really soul-ly underground vibe, and a commercial end of it where anything would go. Then there was the more glam gay scene where people like Sylvester would go and do a live set and he'd be all queened up, standing up on stage, singing *You Make Me Feel* . I love the music, but this guy doesn't do anything for me. Sooner or later, a little bit more funk came into the scene with hip-hop, and then disco sort of took a fall and was replaced with this dark hip-hop style, which sort of lost it for me until house and acid house came along. We could say that acid house was a progression of disco music.

Obviously, you have to do what you believe in as a dj entertaining other people. Trying to realize the potential of that is very difficult. I try not to think about it too much. I tried to play the guitar, the drums, and the piano. I also tried to sing, but I realized I wasn't very good at any of it. I was good as a dj, so I followed that path.

DJ Hell

"Hell" has nothing to do with the devil or hell. I visited this homeopathic astrologer in Berlin before the Love Parade. He explained to me that my pseudonym is in no way connected to hell, but rather to shine, sparkle, and brightness.

International Deejay Gigolos, my label, refers to this whole business that's partly totally removed from real life, where everything's taken care of. You go to a city, they pick you up, they bring you to a hotel, you eat dinner, all of these rituals. You don't have to take care of anything and besides that you earn money, play in the best clubs, which is where the girls are, naturally. All of that gave me the idea to call the label *Gigolo*, this gigolo lifestyle. Or gigoletta, you shouldn't forget that.

Most of the djs are known for the music they produce or play, but I want to go to a club and not know what to expect. The music needs to surprise and excite me and take me in all directions. It's like making love to a woman, it's not always the same position and rhythm. Talk to the ladies, they'll give you the same answer. I'd like to do another twenty years. This music is still so new, it's the first time that djs have been in the spotlight so there should be no limitations with your age. Why should I stop? I think I'll always be a dj. François Kervorkian is my biggest hero, he's 48! I went to see him play at *Body & Soul* (club in New York) last weekend and he was amazing. He really knows how to dj - he plays everything from soulful house to minimal stuff to classic disco. There are not a lot of djs like him. I try to do the same thing but with a different feel. I have a lot of new wave, rock, disco, and electronic influences. My roots go in so many different directions. I couldn't say that I was influenced only by this or that. I am influenced by music in general. That can be *Tuxedomoon*, the early *Residents* stuff, or even Herbert Grönemeyer. Then we listened to *Scritti Politi*. And *Art of Noise* had a lot of good dance mixes that I already played in clubs years ago. I still try to show a lot and not to limit my range. I hope I can show people new ways in order to move everything much more in the direction of pop. I use my old favorites and try to integrate them in a contemporary aesthetics. It's about respect and it's not a Frankenstein method, as some have claimed. It's not like a new way for me; it's how I always sound when I play in a club, when I produce, when I make albums. I've been involved in music for twenty years, so for me this is just a normal set. Sometimes when you play to a bigger crowd, say five thousand people, there's a different kind of atmosphere, so you have to change things a bit. Anyway, it's important not to always play the same records. I have no order in my crate. I react to the moment. A lot of djs go out and have their two-hour sets figured out beforehand and they can't change what they play. I'm not that kind of dj. I'm more versatile.

D ave C lar k e

There's no debate really: techno has always been around and it has influenced everything. It's always being shortchanged. If it gets recognition, great, but if it gets hi-jacked by the wrong people that's not good. Anyway, I tend not to look behind me.

I'm definitely not workshy, and after what I've been through, djing is far less of a hassle than recording. I'll play anywhere people will have me, because I get a massive buzz out of djing and playing decent music. I occasionally play an electro set, which is like my alternative jazz set, but in the main I still play techno because it's still challenging music, whereas djing trance is like tipping your toes into the depths of hell. There's a serious misconception about techno, that people don't want to hear it anymore. Maybe that's the case in the UK, but on the continent it's still the most popular form of dance music. Anyway, even if trance is the music of the moment, do you really think there's only room for one *McDonald's* and no *à-la-carte* restaurants in a town? Ironically, trance evolved from techno during the early 90s, but it hasn't progressed at all since then. Techno is constantly moving forward. Do you really think we'll be able to say the same about today's trance producers in ten years time?

I'm not moody, it's just called a lack of sleep and too much time spent in *British Airways* departure lounges. If I seem unfriendly, it's because it takes me a while to warm up to people. I've got to cut through the bullshit that most djs come out with. I can appreciate it if someone is genuinely trying to be friendly towards me, but most of the time I'm faced with friendliness that immediately smacks of "You're my friend. Now, where can you take my career?" When I get close to someone, I'll help them if they need help. That's what friendship is about: being there for your friends when they really need you, which is completely different from the kind of self-seeking bullshit most people in my profession throw at you.

I want to dj a little bit less anyway because I want to spend more time in the studio; I've done my traveling, really. I still enjoy the djing, but the travel part lost its shine a long time ago. I don't even get excited about the air miles anymore. It's just like commuting, really. It's gotten to the stage where I can immediately recognize an airport when it's on television.

G ree n Vel v et

I started playing the saxophone in elementary school. Then I started experimenting with keyboards while I was studying to become an industrial engineer. After graduation, I did my first internship at a local laboratory and it was immediately obvious to me that this was not my calling. The work was dull and conventional, and I got the chills when I thought about doing that for the rest of my life. When I decided to quit grad school in order to try and make it in music, I thought that somebody would understand but nobody did. I never regretted dropping out of grad school. The only thing that I miss is the problem-solving aspect of my chemical engineering studies. I used to really enjoy that. Producing started off as a hobby during my college days when I loved the sound of house music in the 80s. The sound of house had a short life so I kept up the tradition and bought myself a keyboard, mixer, and drum machine, $90 in all. As for djing, my dad was a dj and he really didn't have an easy life. I always thought that there was no way you could make a living as a dj. I never wanted to

go down that road. I was really fortunate that I knew people in the industry, and that's the main reason why I was able to become successful, I guess.

It's not like I'm Curtis Jones and then all of a sudden Green Velvet just takes over, and I'm a totally different person, and I don't have anything that separates between the two identity-wise. It's not like that. I think it's more of an extension of my personality, and it is who I am, but it's sometimes a bit more dramatic in appearance, but that comes with being a musician. That's just a part of being a musician.

I'm just a house head. I just love house music. My definition of house is a bit more expansive than a lot of other people think. They put a limit to the definition of what house is to them. House is just music that has that 4/4 beat. That can be house, it can be techno, it can be whatever, but for me that's just house, cause that's how I was introduced to it back in the 80s. Back then we had house, but we also listened to what they call industrial or new wave and, of course, disco, but it was all house to me. What I do has the punk attitude, but it's not really punk rock. I know *The Sex Pistols* and *The Ramones* and I have their stuff, but this isn't a retro-punk thing. Because punk has been done a million zillion times. I have taken punk influences—especially the questioning of authority— and added something new to make it sound different. It's punk by electronic means. Punk was just mad at everything and everybody, including itself. That was the beauty of it. But Green Velvet, instead of being like, "Fuck You," is more like, "Why the fuck are you this way." A lot of music is political. It just so happens that you don't hear it in the dance genre very often—but I think it can be done.

35

Art Center College of Design

L   uke S late r

Even when I was just a small kid, I was into music in a strange way. I used to do some weird shit. I wasn't really a "hanging out with people" sort of a kid. We had this piano in my house, and I used to have piano lessons, and I got really bored of those lessons. I don't know what it is, but in England it's becoming like a ritual for kids to have piano lessons. So it slightly tipped my mind about piano lessons. When I got to a certain age, I started thinking, "Well, why am I doing this? I don't really want to learn these pieces of music. I don't really like what I'm playing." I used to take the piano apart and sort of de-tune it. There's three strings for each note. So you get a real fat sort of honky-tonk sound. My dad had this like old reel-to-reel. It's really old, and when you recorded on it, it sounded really kind of warbly. I used to record that weird piano sound and overdub it with any old shit. That's how I grew up. I was in a band when I was 13. I was the drummer. I don't know why I was doing it, actually. But what I do remember was that the keyboarder had an 808 (drum machine) and a *Prophet V* synth. We were at one of these band practices, and he didn't come anymore. So I had to use the 808 for the drums, and I played bits on the synth. He just never turned up to get his gear, and I've still got his 808. That was a change. That was around the same time when electro came to England and it totally changed my life. When I first heard electro in England, it was the first type of music that was dance music but wasn't a song. It had to do with rhythm and noise. It wasn't pop music. There wasn't anything like it at the time. You had stuff like northern soul, but that was still soul; it wasn't electronic. When I heard electronic music, that was it. And I haven't changed at all since then. I believe that the first house tracks were moved on from electro. Not the commercial electro like *Break Machine* and all that *Chaka Khan* business but the real shit. The stuff that had real feeling. The first house was made from the same machines. The thing is that there was so much shit music on the 80s. There was so much commercial drum-machine nonsense that had no groove, but electro was hard and metallic. It was cold, but it was funky. That's always been the thing for me that you can have an attitude in a record, but it can still be funky. That's why those records are important to me. When they were making those records, they didn't copy anything. I've always wanted to try and feel like that when I've been making records. The whole acid thing was pretty intense and it was really about underground music. Suddenly, there were people in Britain that decided to go a different way in everything. Not many people knew about it; there were a few little clubs in London and it was all going off. Suddenly, blokes weren't killing each other, they weren't glassing each other and fighting for all the girls. People were just having a good time. And that was really refreshing, because before that I didn't go out. I didn't dj, I didn't want to go the sort of clubs where the dj plays Luther Vandross crooners. I thought, "Fucking hell, this is shit, man." And then when this whole club thing developed, it was like I've found my home. So I think it has a lot of influence on what I do now, but I don't think of it as of something I want to keep.

It was about '87 and we were going to go meet this bloke down in a club in London who was setting up a label. We wanted to put stuff out; it was a club called *The Sound Shaft* , which was mixed with a gay club called *Heaven*. We walked in there and there was this dj in there whose name was Steve Bell. He was mixing records. I thought "That would be me." So I made some mix tapes, gave it to the blokes around the club, and I ended up playing down there every week for a year. We just wanted to put out a lot of records, because there was nothing out there, especially in Britain. When we started in Britain, getting our records sold and played was the hardest thing in the world, because the media used to be so silky and smooth. We were coming out with all the hard stuff and everything, and it was a bit odd to hear stuff like that, but we didn't care. We were making records to play in clubs, for me to play and for the clubs that were happening.

You've got to have those edgy bits, you've got to have the whole thing, you can't just be happy the whole time. You've got to have a bit of depression, and I thought, "No one's really saying that, everyone is saying you've got to be like this sort of happy person all the time," and I'm thinking, "No one's like that, no one's happy all the time." If you ignore your other emotions, it just makes you ill. I like the weird and slightly on the edge, not quite socially acceptable things in life. Music can be whatever you want. If people tell me that this isn't the done thing to do and it doesn't fit in this scene or that, then it makes me want to do it even more. I've never made any rules about how to do things. It's just not that complicated with me. I think the hardest barrier is when you become well-known or established by something you've already done. You need to clear your mind of everything before you go into the studio. Otherwise you become a cliché of what you've already done. It may turn on some people, but it bores me.

C ari L eke bus c h

In the early 80s, I started with the records my mother was collecting, just like everybody else. I found some records that I really liked. I found some old stuff from groups like *Kraftwerk*. When I was around 11-12 years old, I started to realize that I liked synthetic and synthesizer sounds better than orthodox guitar sounds, for instance. I started collecting records that had that new feeling to them. In the 80s, a lot of those records came out. All the way up to Africa Bambaata, they listened to *Kraftwerk* and stuff like that. There are so many groups and records, too many to mention. We had a record store in Stockholm at the time, which had really good access to an American distributor, so we had all the early stuff from New York, Chicago, and Detroit. I started to buy all that stuff. That was around '85-'86, then came Chicago House, the *Trax* history, acid house and so on. Around the same time, I started buying my first equipment. I had some friends with synthesizers, so we started to mess around a bit. It was fun. I had a friend in the 4th, 5th, and 6th grade, and he had some stuff at home. He was pretty smart because he had already built his own synthesizers at the age of 10. I was pretty impressed by that. We were playing around with all that and I thought, "This is mad fun!" I guess in a way he helped me realize that I had to buy myself one of those toys. I started to save money. The prices were massive. I could never imagine that one day I would own one of these things, because it's so expensive, especially in Sweden. I guess if you have really rich parents, you can ask them, but that wasn't the case. I started to work in an amusement park to save money and bought my first synthesizers.

I had my own club in the late 80s. I think we did most parties in '89, at least ten. That went of pretty well; we got something started there. There were some other promoters in Stockholm, all around the age of 18 to 20. We all started doing parties, and people attended those parties, because we were playing a new kind of sound. We were the pioneers in Stockholm. Nobody had done anything like that before us. I guess the techno community in Sweden nowadays has some recognition, but there wasn't anything going on before. Everything was very underground and still is. You can't just say, "I wanna go to a techno party tonight," because there won't be one. Since Stockholm is a pretty small city, and the scene for techno isn't too big, we all bump into each other sooner or later. I met Adam Beyer at a party of a mutual friend. He was playing some of his own tracks on the stereo. I was like, "What is this all about?" He came up to me and said it was his own stuff, and I answered that I was doing the same thing. He knew me because he had already seen me play. Immediately, we had something in common. So I met all those guys. It's really a small group of people in Stockholm who produce. We listen to the same stuff, and we all have been working in the same record store called *Planet Rhythm*.

It's just cold and dark in Stockholm for the better part of the year, so you'll be in the studio. You get a lot of studio time and peace and quiet. I used to produce massive loads of tracks. Out of a hundred tracks, I maybe do ten really good ones, but I release fifty anyway. I think it's important not only to release this pop-chart material where everything has to be just perfect. I think it's more important to adapt a different attitude to releasing tracks. You should be able to release some tracks that probably won't work on the dance floor, but you know they work well with something else. You can't do something totally new every time you release something. Sometimes you have to take a couple of steps backwards in order to get a couple of steps ahead for the next release. I have my formulas and patterns. When I don't have a good idea to start with, I always have a pattern that I start with. That can be anything. I can start working with my reel tape for example, making weird loops and playing them backwards, whatever. Then you've got *Cubase* on the computer and hard-disc recording systems, and you can use that in different ways. I kind of like to loop stuff on my drum machines. You put them on tape, then in the computer, back and forth, until you have some nice structures.

I'm totally independent; I own most of my tracks. If you have a massive contract with a major label, you can get into sticky situations. When it comes to the music, sounds, and the visual things, I like to do it myself.

Adam Beyer

It's a bit odd in Sweden. The scene is very special as there are a great number of Swedish producers and labels doing very well abroad. However, we don't really have a proper local club scene. I can't really get a grip on what people are into. Maybe because I don't go to parties here. Music-wise, there's a lot of labels coming up, a lot of good ones, but also some that I can't find any concept or thought behind. It's more like, "Let's do a label for a laugh." I think people should be a bit more aware of what they release. For a city like this, it's tragic that we don't have one decent house and techno club with good djs. In the rest of the world, a lot of stuff is happening and a lot of new territories are opening up. A lot of the eastern countries are picking up too, especially through the Internet and mp3, since they can't afford vinyl. America has got a huge market, and the kids are really getting into electronic music over there. I feel that techno is far from dead (which is something media always says).

So far , I've been very focused on music to use when I'm djing. I'm a dj from the beginning, and sometimes I don't even consider myself a producer in that sense. It's more like I'm creating pieces and tools for djs. But it's something I want to start to change. I don't think I'm really satisfied with anything I've done, to be honest. I've been close a couple of times, but I've always felt I could have done better. But that's the thing with techno: it can never be complete, there's always room for more.

I always tend to use my sampler a lot. It has always been the main piece of equipment, even more than before. I used to be into analog synths and stuff, but I feel that they are getting very limited in their performance. I'm also getting into using more software lately. It's incredible what you can do with a computer these days.

Basically, remixes are a good thing, but only if you do something new with the track and find your own definition of the idea behind the track. As long as you don't do a remix just for it's own sake, but in order to show new aspects, it's ok. But as soon as it's only about the money, I think it's crap. And I don't like djs who are so sentimental that they only play old classics. I want to go on. Progress. Just play the latest records. Of course, there are good old tracks that still sound fresh and that you can play now and then. But the rest is sentimental crap and I am not into that.

Ke nn y L a r k i n

I have been interested in music my whole life. Everything from classical to jazz and everything in between. I have always had an ear for music. Since I was little, I was able to listen to a record and peck on the piano the melodies I heard in the songs. Formally, I never took any lessons, but I started fooling around with music in '85, when I bought a little tiny *Casio* keyboard and tried to duplicate house music, which was very easy to do. I got into house music through Terrence Parker. We went to high school together and he was a dj. He had this weird music that hardly nobody in our school got into, except for the few who picked up on the spiritual vibe the music provided through its repetitive, hypnotic nature. I went to the airforce in '86 with house music as my way of life, musically, and in '88 I got out and came home to an entirely different scene happening in Detroit. There was another type of music emerging, or that had already emerged while I was away, and I immediately took to it. Derrick May had a mix show on Detroit's main black radio station, and even though I didn't know him at the time or his music, I knew that the music he mixed was the kind of music I wanted to do. The music that he played I later found out

was from Detroit. I think a lot of people doing this music, or any music, have to look into the future and decide where they would like to go with their music. If that is ultimately with major labels and remixing, fine, they have fulfilled their dreams. Why should we condemn that? The problem lies in compromising who they are and what their music is about. Personally, I feel that sounds do play a big role in the music, but it is how the sound is used that is more important. That is what keeps Detroit on the edge. That completely different, innovative way on how we go about making our music. With the deluge of techno artists from all over the world making headlines, it's easy (although very wrong) to forget that techno was created in Detroit, Michigan, by African-Americans.

A lot of styles of music come out in my moods: jazz, house, it depends on how I'm feeling. A lot of my music is improvised. I just start playing chords and get emotions off that, and then I just go. All this 180 bpm shit is not how techno was. People like the early Detroit guys and *Kraftwerk* were showing people their emotions through their music. That's what I'm doing as well.

Miss Kittin & the Hacker

In general, I get inspiration from everything and everybody around me: a woman in the bus, my Yoga teacher, my cats, the book I'm reading … But I never tried to go into the same direction as someone else, like I had an idol. But if I had to choose someone, I would definitely say Madonna. I admire her, that's all. I love Frank Sinatra and the American crooners and romantic jazz in general.

The Hacker prepares loops at home in Grenoble. When I go there, we build the track together and when he's making the balance, I write my lyrics. Then we make a test and we often record the track in one shot. It has to be quickly done and fresh; if not, it's not fun and no good. It has to be something funny or ironic, because it will make us laugh a lot. You can get the inspiration for a track while hanging out at the studio or while djing at a party. I am not just a "voice"—I am hard working girl who doesn't make things easy for herself. We have enough complicity not to interfere too much with the role of the other and that's great because we are independent from each other. As a live act, every trip with the Hacker is funny. We had a lot of bad gigs and non-professional attitudes from technicians, stuff missing and so on. We like to be ironic. I think people like this ironic stuff because in some ways they recognize themselves in the lyrics. We don't like to think about any intellectual meaning, though. We just want to have fun. The Hacker was in a new wave band before, and for him our duo is like a dream come true. He's found a girl to sing and he feels like the man in the dark behind his keyboards. Like *Soft Cell* or something.

In a live set, all the tracks are done. We can't modify them, there's no surprise for us, but there are the improvisations I can develop with the audience. But I have much more fun playing records. I have done it for 6 years now, and I can take risks, record after record: you develop something in 2 hours instead of playing something planned in 30 minutes during a live set. In a live, you also have to play a role, with all your body, but as a dj, I'm totally myself and I'm proud of it. I don't like to play roles. I am far away from a kind of star status but I live the music. Sadly enough, there's still not enough women in the music business who are involved at the top. Djing is my passion, it's my first job. I prefer it to working in the studio. Djing is how I make my living. It's very egotistical as I have a lot of fun doing it. But even when I have great time doing it, I never forget who I am playing for. The audience in a club pays for my living with their cover charge. Still, you should take risks and not just play what people already know—that would be too simple and basically pretty boring. Who cares whether it's techno, house, or electro?! I think it's a question of age how you deal with this. When you're very young, you're much more exclusive, you're very much into a certain style. But the older and more mature you get, the more open you become. Everything else would be pretty monotonous after all.

Ellen Allien

Initially, I didn't want to become a dj. I just wanted to be on stage and juggle or hang on the trapeze. But I never wanted to be a dj, although music was always around. For four years, I lived in a music studio with my then boyfriend who was into soul and funk. Myself, I played the saxophone. I did my training as an acrobat for 1 1/2 years and hung out in studios where musicians practiced. I sang a bit and basically tried out everything. It was in a squat where everyone did something in that vein. I was in the midst of it and tried out everything without wanting to be professional. The stuff you do when you're 18. In '92, I worked at the bar of the *Fischlabor* (Berlin club) to pay for my training as an acrobat. They had djs there. One day, I jokingly asked whether they would let me dj. Achim, a friend of mine, said, "Sure, go for it!" I started to get seriously interested in music and to buy records. I got my first gigs at the *Bunker*. This was the first club where I got harder and more experimental. Before I used to play house and ambient. And one day I was asked whether I wanted to do a radio show on *Kiss FM* (Berlin radio station). After house and ambient, I started to play experimental trance. Now I am sort of in the middle, experimental in any case, a mix of house and techno. I don't play retro-80s stuff, too trite, and minimal techno, too intellectual. You can't pigeonhole me. I buy what I like.

As a female dj, you're naturally exotic. But you only get taken seriously if you develop your own sound. My label is called *Bpitch Control* because I always liked the word "bitch." After all, I grew up at the *Metropol* (Berlin club) during the Hi-NRG era. Back then, there were a lot of tracks with the word "bitch." As a woman I thought that the pun was funny: to me, the dj is the bitch who pitches and controls people. As a dj, you work with people; you don't just egocentrically do your own thing. We get paid and we have to do our act. And that's why people love us. Moreover, there's always something sexual about music. In my sets, there's not just this sound or that sound. It changes. That's very important to me. Because that's Berlin. Berlin to me means undefined spaces and freedom. There's no censorship. As far as I'm concerned, there's no "intelligent music." Every sound has its justification. Every sound does something for someone. If I ask myself, "How did he do it?" when I hear a certain sound, does that make it intelligent? No, it just makes it interesting. I am more grown up now. I see producing as my motor and my outlet. It used to be djing, working for the radio, and clubbing. That changed. Most happens when I am in the studio. That's how I can best express myself. Between '92 and '94, everyone in techno said that we don't need lyrics. Certainly not love and peace. Because we feel that through the music. A certain sound, for instance a *Moog*, expressed so much that it was enough for us. Today, I listen to these techno tools and no one talks about love. But love's the most important thing. People always say that it has no relation to techno. But that's not true to me. Romanticism is very important to me. Not just a type of sound that gives you a quick kick that is gone after a short while. For me, language is part of it, too. Otherwise, it gets too abstract because everyone can think what they want. Basically, I want that the things I feel are transported to listener. Most people don't even dare to be romantic, or happy, or sad anymore. I think it's important to live out all of this.

Th o mas   S c h u h m   a   c   he   r

I djed for the first time in junior high. It was a class party. For days, I compiled tapes with a friend of mine. We had endless debates about order, content, and appearances. And then it was suddenly real: 30 class mates, I was insecure and nervous, drank way too much liquor. As an opener *Bigmouth Strikes Again* by *The Smiths*. No one dances. More liquor and some beer. Now it's *The Normal*'s *Warm Leatherette*. What's the matter with the girls, why doesn't anything happen there? Then *Kwa Liga* by *The Residents* and on with *Boys Don't Cry* by *The Cure*. And then I immediately realized: remain behind the tape decks, just continue, feel the atmosphere, find your own flow, just don't leave. And all of a sudden, I had this incredible feeling that I still love so much, that I wouldn't want miss. And yet, I can't precisely describe it.

In the mid-80s, there was hip-hop: *Public Enemy*, *Eric B. & Rakim*, *Run DMC*. These beats, all the samples, and, of course, the rapping. It's music that I like to this day. I then had my scooter phase. I never owned one, but I liked the atmosphere, the girls, the music at runs and all-night parties. Soul, that is. At that time, I listened to EBM, mainly *Nitzer Ebb*, but also *Front 242* and *Skinny Puppy*. In '89, all these techno productions from Frankfurt came out that,

in comparison to EBM, were much more clearly produced for clubs, for discos. At the latest, this was the point where I noticed my preference for dance-able electronic music. In spite of the aggression and energy that I liked about EBM, I liked the four-to-the floor rhythm and the bass lines in these Frank-furt techno productions much better. In '89, I experienced my first techno party at *Dorian Gray* (Frankfurt club). These basses! Incredibly intense. Until then I had djed at my own EBM parties that I had organized with a friend. It was clear to me that the sound at our parties would change now. In December '89, we organized the first party where I played techno. The thing with tech house, that is techno house, started for me around '91. It has remained with me in my way of producing music. House in this context doesn't mean classical traditional house, but rather techno with a soul aspect, a deeper level. It stands in contrast to the monotonous loop-driven, "hey ho, let's go" techno, that some call "Schranz," which personally think is horrible.

Every week I buy a lot of records, whether it's reggae, drum 'n' bass, or hip-hop. I am interested in everything and I get ideas from everything. When I hear a cool bass line, I imagine how I would transform that in a club context. Sometimes I just sit behind my synthesizer and experiment. I love to program sounds. A lot of good ideas are generated that way, in particular those with a cross-over potential. Or I hear a great sample, or loop, on a record that I start to work with and go on from there. Because of my long experience, I know where a track is going when I hear a certain sound. There's a lot of producers who just combine thousands of different sounds that might sound good by themselves, but don't fit together. That's where I have a pretty good overview.

Der Dritte Raum

I had to learn the piano when I was little, although I did not want to. Of course, it now helps, but the pressure wasn't good. My father wanted me to learn it. I started to, but then I could luckily get away. After 2 or 3 years, I stopped. The first instrument I played of my own free will was a synthesizer, a *Korg MS-10*. My father still says that I am not making music. He thinks it's great that I make records, but he doesn't accept the music itself. Music made with synthesizers and drum computers isn't music to him. His father probably tore away his *Blue Note* records when he started to listen to jazz. I guess that's what happens in every generation. I used to build radios. My father probably reacted so heavily against it that I just had to do it. I thought it was much more exciting to sit in attic soldering radio transistors than to do homework. That's how I got into synthesizers. Today, when I dislike certain functions in a machine, I just rebuild them. With analogue machines, at least, that's no big deal.

The idea behind the live sets with my co-pilot Ralf Uhrland is the jam session. We take our machines and tracks with us—we don't just play *Der Dritte Raum*, we also play Ralf's solo tracks and unrelelased material—and then we simply mix. It constantly changes. We work with two independent mix systems that are neither linked nor synced, with one *Powerbook* each and 1-2 synthesizers on the rack. That's how we mix, like djs with their decks. While one plays, we reload the other and then we start and pitch. We mix on a 24-channel desk; that's 12 channels each with the single sounds, like bass, snare, hi-hat, 303 (drum machine), and so on. It's fucking close to a dj-mix. Shortly before our set, we discuss what and at what speed we're going to play. At some freaked-out acid party, though, we might play for three hours without having thought about it in advance. But when you play at a rave and you only have half an hour, you have to have an agreement about what you are going to do.

I am interested in the cross-over of noises, vocals, nature, and instruments, to combine these elements in a structured way. The thrill is in the arrangement. That's exactly were music starts. The single sound is studio technology. You can describe that in technical terms, there's algorhythms, whatever. It's just a sound. But if it floors you, it's been rhythmically or melodically (i.e. musically) well-placed. I have never made film music, but I'm interested in it. I might do something like that one day. I am very interested in film as a medium. I used to experiment with a video camera. It's very similar to me; there's not that many differences. The technology is almost the same whether you make music with a hard-disk recording system or whether you make videos on an *Avid* system. The difference is that in film you conceive and arrange a scene, whereas in music you edit different sounds together. In both film and music you arrange a sequence in time, you freeze a slice of life, you want to spellbind people and lead them out of their everyday reality.

S l am

Glasgow's an old industrial town, which is still very obvious. There used to a lot of shipyards, but now it's more service-industry oriented. Recently, there's been a strong rejuvenation. Today, people are very friendly and open, similar to Liverpool or Ireland. There's a healthy club scene and you can go out on Tuesdays and Wednesdays, too. We just do what we believe in. We don't have to look to London for that. It's all so stylish there and there's a new hype every two or three months. It's should be refreshing, but in the end there's no real progress.

When we started, *Trax Records* appeared and all of those acid house and Detroit-techno things probably influenced us most. We produced our first track in '91. We only had the most basic equipment, but we wanted to make the step from listening to producing. So we just went on the studio and recorded our first single with us on one side and *Rejuvenation* on the other. From there, the whole thing grew slowly, first in the UK and much later on the continent. We were the first independent dance label in Scottland. Strictly dub, that's what we want to work on more often in the future. Although it's basically narrow-minded to like only one style. It's mostly an image thing. If you want to pursue a certain style, you can easily do it with a 12". But there has to be more to an album. We also listen to a lot of things that have nothing to do with techno or dance: soundtracks, jazz, obscure pop. It's not that we're against vocals in general, but the right feeling's got to be there. Not like in the US, "Ooh, saw you last nite ... Miss you so." If you're going to have vocals, you got to have a message.

When we did remixes for *Brand New Heavies*, Jean-Michel Jarre, *The Orb*, or *Stereo MC's*, for instance, we basically wrote new tracks for them. The problem was that some of them did not want to be remixed by us. But we needed the money to build our studio. Now we just do remixes of things we're really convinced of. The most unnerving thing about remixing is that you have to follow someone else's schedule.

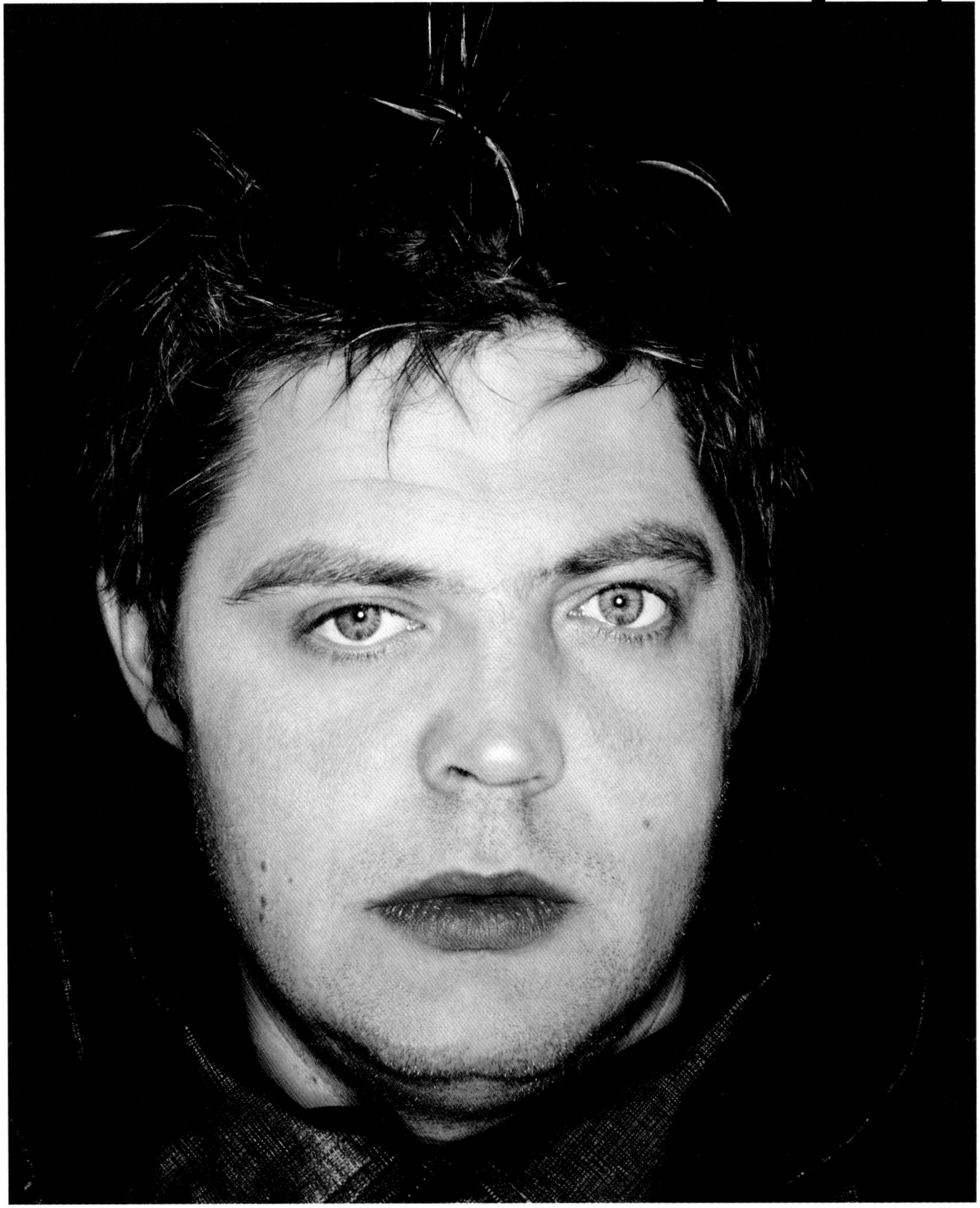

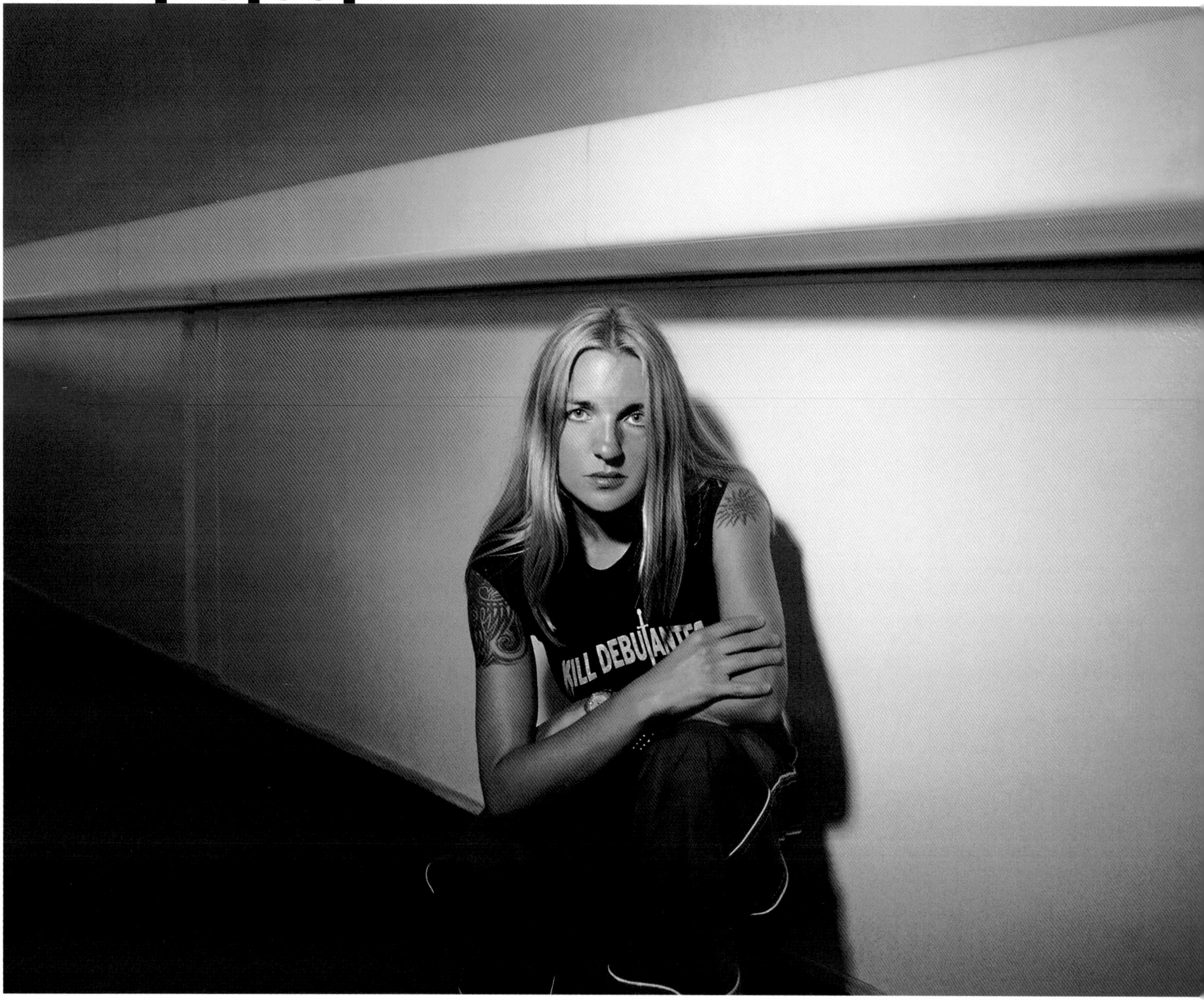
KILL DEBUTANTES

M i s s   D j a   x

I was born and raised in the center of Eindhoven, a mid-size industrial town in the south of the Netherlands. At the age of 9, I bought my first record. It was a single by *The Beatles*. It cost only seventy-five cents and had a white sleeve with a hole in the middle. I didn't like the sleeve so I painted a colorful flower on it. Soon I started spending all my pocket money on records. Nowadays my collection contains over 7'000 records. For my 13th birthday I got a light organ. I painted the ceiling of my room black (my mum didn't like this but when she found out, it was already done), and I imagined that I was the dj in a discotheque. At that time, I realized that I wanted to become a dj, either at a radio station or at a club. At the age of 16, I left school and home at the same time. I rented a room in a student's house in the center of Eindhoven and got a job as a dj in a club. In those days, instead of being considered a pop star, a dj was seen as a kind of living jukebox. I found myself a job in a clothing store that also sold records. I really wanted to work in the record department, but I had to work in the clothing department because only boys could work in the record department. Of course, I didn't work there for long. Luckily, I found a job at a record store. I ended up working there for 8 years, then I found a job as an export manager at dance distributor. I was still playing at various clubs until I received the first requests for international gigs in '91.

All kinds of musicians brought their demo tapes to the record store. Among those tapes I found such interesting material that I did not understand why no one paid attention to it. I thought, "Damn, isn't there anybody out there who is sensitive to good music?" I decided to do it myself and founded *Djax Records*. Everybody told me I was crazy, but I believed in it. Besides, those reactions were one more reason to go on. I devote myself to the things I believe in. Whether I can make money with it doesn't matter to me. If I think an act has quality, I'll sign it. Period. There are quite a lot of artists busying themselves with underground music but hardly any serious outlets. There are major and independent labels but not much in between. At independent companies, it's fairly easy to release a record. If need be, you can even found a company yourself. But in most cases there is no money left for publicity. So artists are not able to work on it seriously and short-lived stars are born. To me, that is the ultimate sense of freedom: not having to mind what the great mass of people may or may not like. The commercial world is extremely stressed—I cannot help the idea that someone is always panting at my neck. Like, "We don't have much time. You should play the very latest, otherwise you'll fall behind." I cannot stand that.

Looking the clothes the women, but also the men wear, or should I say don't wear, at those parties, it goes pretty far. The nice thing about it is that despite this no one gets molested. It's one of the few scenes where this is still possible. In this case, eroticism isn't self-evidently put on a level with physical love. Besides, this is not exactly what those evening are all about. People don't come in search of sex. Although there are super-sexy djs. The way they play and move their muscular bodies to the bass sounds combined with the feeling of black disco. That's rather lascivious. But my music, which is a bit harder, heavier, and cooler, does not lend itself to this purpose.

Dave Angel

I was born in London Chelsea in '66. My mother was a housewife and my father was a jazz musician. My first musical instrument was a drum at the age of eight. It made me feel just wicked to be alive, and I could just escape whatever shit was happening. I didn't get on well with school and spent little time there, preferring truancy to chemistry and the music room to the classroom. My uncle had a reggae sound system, so I was always into the one-turntable side of djing. I must have been around 11 or 12 years old. When I was around 15, a group of friends and myself got together our own little sound system, playing mainly for free at little parties. When I was 20, I auditioned for *Phase 1* radio, which was one of the leading pirates at the time of the acid house explosion, and I was really excited when I got the slot. Before that, my father had given me the first turntable that I ever had; it was a *Garrard* belt-drive thing, so it was no good for mixing. I didn't know anything about mixing at that time anyway, so I was happily plugging away, pretending to be a radio dj with one *Garrard* deck. A few years later, it broke and my then girlfriend who is now my wife bought me a *Technics 1210*. At this point I wanted to learn how to mix. So I traded my favorite leather jacket for a *Marantz* turntable; it wasn't great but at least it had a pitch control. I spent endless hours practicing by myself until I got it right.

When I began playing with different people, it was awesome, and all of a sudden we were creating this music by ourselves. When the whole techno thing hit me, it was just too much. I thought, "Man, I gotta get in on this." It was always difficult before that, because I was relying on the people whom I made music with. With technology, I no longer had the other hassles. If I wanted a bass line, then bang, I could create one, or if I wanted another beat, again, I could do what I wanted. Everything went mad with the technology around '87 and I started producing. My first production was a remix of the *Eurythmics* track *Sweet Dreams*. There was no specific strategy behind me doing that track. I had beats and a bass line and a riff, and then I looked through my records and pulled out that track. When I bootlegged it, the track got so much attention that the next minute I had lawyers from *BMG* out looking for me. But thankfully I got put into a real recording studio with Dave Dorrell and the *Sweet Dreams Nightmare Mix* was made. And I got a nice check. And

suddenly, I was a producer as well as a dj. It did pretty well in the charts—number 23, my highest so far—but I have never made a record just to make a hit. I make records because I enjoy it, but it is also about you getting paid. I never bootlegged another track and now that I know the proper channels I wouldn't do it again. But you should do anything once. I've always seen remixing as kind of like a lucky thing. Doing the *Eurythmics*, I took it upon myself and did this. I wasn't asked to do it. But having your office phone ring and you've got Prince on the other end of the line saying he wants me to do a remix: just think what a surprise that would be. Remixing and producing are just the same. If I remix a track, I'm injecting my production into it, sometimes it is all my own production with just one sample from the original.

That success gave me the drive and confidence to start producing bolder tracks and that in turn set me on the path to defining my own sound. It's true, the whole Detroit thing has certainly been an influence, but it's by no means restricted me to one vibe. Listening to the stuff that was coming out of Detroit in the early 90s, you can really hear the rhythms and melodies and you can pinpoint where it has come from. The kind of music I play is, in a nutshell, funky. To me, a good gig is when you have a good sound system with a really up-for-it crowd. The downside to it all is lots of late nights and a messed-up body clock. When I'm on the road, I tend to stay in my hotel room with my laptop, chopping up loops and using them as scratchpads or templates for new tracks. This is my relaxation.

59

Claude Young

Growing up in Detroit was somehow strange. My parents separated when I was really, really young. I first lived with my mother right in the city. When I went to high school, I moved to the suburbs. And then back to the city. Suburbs, city, suburbs, city, always back and forth. Quite crazy. Detroit is just Detroit. You grow up there and you have to deal with the city the way it is. There are really bad neighborhoods, it can be really violent. But when you're confronted with it on an everyday basis, you become somehow immune. At certain point, you just don't care about the violence anymore.

My parents are the biggest influence and inspiration in regards to my musical career. As a young boy, I remember going to *WJLB* where my father was a radio dj and sitting in on his shows. It was so fascinating to me, all the buttons, lights, cart and reel-to-reel machines. My dad was the first black dj to play a wide variety of music on the radio in Detroit (contrary to what others may claim). At home (as well as on the radio) I heard everything from David Bowie to *Kraftwerk* to *Parliament* to Miles Davis to *New Order* to *Run DMC*. I think he was lucky to be a dj in an era when you could play anything you liked on air, and the dj really did have all the power. Not like now where everything is programmed by some idiot who has no a clue about music, but has season tickets to all the sporting events, courtesy of all the major record labels. Originally, I had no intention of going into the music business, I was studying TV production in school and wanted to be a TV producer/editor. Our high school had a radio station and I had two after-school shows. The first was a 50s and 60s show. My second weekly show was called *20 Minutes Into the Future*. This was definitely more electronic. I played *Nitzer Ebb*, *Front 242*, *New Order*, *Black Flag*, *Inner City*, *Kraftwerk*, anything I thought had an edge to it. When I got a job at *WHYT*, I started as an intern, answering request-line phones and doing market research. One day, I was called into the music director's office, and he asked me to give him a mix demo. They wanted to change the line-up for their Saturday-night mix show and were looking new talent. There were three places for shows and I got one of them. I had a two-hour mix show. The first hour I played commercial stuff. Basically anything that was on the station play list. My second hour was a mixture of local and import tech- no, *Metroplex*, *Underground Resistance*, *Warp*, and so on. I got into a lot of trouble with the station manager because he said no one wanted to hear an hour of instrumentals. He had no fucking clue about music.

I was in a record shop one day looking for locally produced music, and I rang some of the labels to see if I could get some promo records for my show. I called *Metroplex* one afternoon, and Anthony "Shake" Shakir answered the phone. He was a big fan of my father's radio show, so we became friends. Shake introduced me to Octave One, Jay Denham, Kevin Saunderson and the rest of the crew. As I was good at two-track tape editing, I began to get called in to do re-edits of recordings for many different artist. The editing led to remix work, and it all snowballed from there. Wanting to make music was a natural progression from editing music. I have always been a technology fanatic, so anything that got me closer to understanding the sound process was a necessity to learn. Something that I think is very much lacking at the moment in dance/techno music, is human creativity (e.g. funk). I don't mean decks and effects or anything like that, I mean a man and two turntables going all out and being creative. Pushing myself to the limits and trying to create a sonic soundscape, not just blending 30 similar records with similar beats. To be honest, if something doesn't happen soon, techno (or what some people now call techno) will be just like trance, full of non-talented wankers playing in Ibiza and making a fortune. Of course, not all techno is like this, but in most of the places I get booked to play at, I can only play a certain type of music. If I try to change, or drop something funky or slower, the people just don't get it. I love jazz music but it is just one part of the spectrum. I am listening to a lot of Cuban music at the moment. I like music where I can feel some kind of sincerity from the players/producers. I don't know what the future will bring, but that is the true beauty of the future. I hope we (producers as a music community) don't spend the next 10 years trying to recreate records that sound as if they were recorded in the 70s. Influence is one thing but mimicking is a waste of time, anyone with tracing paper can call themselves an artist. The true artist makes something from nothing.

Unfortunately, music history is repeating itself in America. Young Americans have a hard time accepting that techno/electronic music was a mostly black-music art form in the beginning. The inability of many young American kids to accept this fact has led the US electronic-music scene to mutate into a marketing playground for corporate clubbing (*Ministry of Sound*, *Home*, *Cream*, etc.). I have spent the majority of my career playing around the world and not much time playing in my own home country due to politics and ignorance. Like Miles Davis and all the other great black musicians of their day, I feel forced to leave my homeland to be appreciated for my work. It's an awful truth but the truth none the less.

Misstress Barbara

I played drums with the cadets. Using the experience I'd had on the snare drum, I took up drumming in my spare time. I bought a big kit for my home. It was beautiful. I was playing the drums with friends in bands and doing a bit of teaching; back then I used to hate electronic music. I didn't know about techno and house, I just knew about commercial dance music. I was a rocker: purple jeans, Doc Marten's, leather jacket, you name it. *Led Zeppelin* were my favorites, and in my CD collection there were *Guns & Roses* and *Iron Maiden*.

One night, when I was 17, I went to a friend's birthday. She wanted to go to a disco so I went with a crowd of people. This club was really commercial and the dj played rock, reggae, cheese, and then half an hour of the latest underground music. I was stood at the bar, drinking my beer, looking at my watch. I couldn't wait to get out. But I was moving my knees. My friend came up to me and was like, "Barbara, you really like house." I was like, "What the hell is house?" He told me what it was. I was like, "Okay, maybe I do," and he told me to go check out raves, parties, and gay clubs because they played house there. And I did. I started going out to these parties and I found out electronic music was different from the *Rhythm Of The Night* shit they played in that club. By '95, I couldn't have fun unless I was trainspotting the dj and seeing what he was doing. I wouldn't even dance anymore.

In February '96, I finally got my turntables. I had to sell my drum kit to afford them. That was one of the biggest heartbreaks in my life, but I came to the conclusion that I wasn't selling the drums to fund a hobby, I was selling them to kick off my career. After two weeks, I offered my first mix tape to that guy Neerav. He didn't want to hear it cause he didn't want to tell me that it probably sucked. I went mad but he invited me to jam with him a couple of weeks later. He was gob-smacked. He took me by my shoulders and looked me in the eyes and said, "You're going to go fucking far". My first gig came three months later. I didn't practice that much. And I still don't. I hate to play in front of a wall. I started djing and started producing a year later while I was still in school, which was in the beginning of '98. At that time, I was inspired by Adam Beyer and Marco Carola more than anyone else. Apart from those two, I was into all the Swedish music: I used to send my demos to Swedish labels because my music would not really fit anywhere else. I also love house and I have always been very inspired by Ian Pooley. I work very hard and have a lot of determination. However, if my music doesn't reach a big audience, it's probably because my music doesn't really have vocals, melodies, or big breakdowns. I could do music like that, but I don't. I don't because it doesn't move me as much. I play on three turntables, mix really fast, and play loads of records in one set. I've been told that I make love to the mixer, as I keep on touching the buttons and twisting all the knobs non-stop. In fact, I am very technical and my hands are always doing something.

The current state of techno world-wide is very sad. I travel to a lot of different cities and countries, and I encounter people who say they don't like techno. But then I play and after my set I get the same people coming up to me saying, "What were you playing? It was amazing!" and when I say, "Well, I played techno." The reaction is always, "That's impossible! I hate techno and I absolutely loved your set!" The problem is that what scares people off techno is the actual word, more than anything else! This happens all the time because most people think that this style of music is mean and hard and dark and fast! It is repetitive, though, and this is why most people don't like it, but techno can be so funky and groovy.

I'm not happy just because I made it in a male-oriented scene and I never think about it. Sure, I have encountered and still come across situations where I feel like I'm not being treated like I deserve to be, or where I'm not getting what I want, and it is probably because there's some sexism involved, but it doesn't stop me and I am certainly not the type of person that will moan about it or become bitter about it. I do my thing and, at the end of the day, I think I've succeeded.

Pascal F. E.O. S.

Minimal sound was always my thing. Sometimes I also play tech and dub house. Sometimes I even like to play at ambient parties. That's important, because this way I can show people that there's not only one type of music. I am not a classic entertainer. When people stand in front of the dj desk and look at what I do, I think it's nice, but I am not really getting a kick out of it. The hype's ok, but I don't need adoration. I think it's great when the evening's beautiful and people enjoy it. After each set, I examine myself. How did people react? Have I made any mistakes? People said it was great, but I thought it sucked. When I make a mistake in my set, it really annoys me. I analyze everything I do three or four times. Maybe that's going to drive me insane one day. I am a perfectionist. In producing in particularl I would never hand in anything I didn't like 100 percent.

When I am in the studio with someone and I have an idea and he has an idea and I like the idea and set it in a relation to my stuff, so what? Because I am sitting in front of the computer and record most things, you just hear that this is F.E.O.S.. I just have my own style. To somehow tinker around and create a musical hodge-podge is nothing. It's difficult to try out every approach and people consequently expect a lot. If you suddenly do a break-beat track, you measure yourself against people who have been doing this for years.

You can't always follow people's tastes when you dj. When that happens, I try to turn it around most of the time. I think you also learn from experience. Like when you had less of an overview of records, you had a problem every evening. When they weren't properly sorted and you didn't know any records, you had to listen to every record. That can really drive you crazy. When that kind of thing happened, I knew I was spending too much time in the studio. That didn't work. Ever since, Friday's the day when I buy records, listen to them, and sort my boxes, because I check what's in them before every gig. Because when I dj for six hours, I want to offer more than a 140 bpm program. Even when there's only two people on the dance floor, djing can be a lot of fun. And if they like it, I could go on for ten more hours, just because I like it. When I come home after an after-hours party and I record a tape, I have sweat on my brows and I want the mix to work perfectly without any mistakes. Anyone who doesn't know this feeling will never know what it means to be a dj. When I have a new record in my hands, I feel a tingle. I have to make tapes every week and I've done that for more than 15 years. When this sensation never lets you go, you know that you still have fun doing it. You really feel it. I mean, two weeks of vacation should actually really kill you. Some collect sculptures, I collect records. I wouldn't want to give away a single track. If I want to hear something one more time and the record's not around, I become quite unbearable.

R ic ar d o Vi ll a - l o b o s

To me, Detroit is a kind of music in which technological possibilities meet rhythms that come from Africa. These rhythms, just like melodies, can lie in between dark and bright worlds; they can be positively or negatively influenced.

These huge enthusiastic clubs, like the Omen in Frankfurt, are dead. People went there out of enthusiasm and that is over. To me, the most important is a feeling of bass and rhythm. It completely takes you over, because you cannot but dance as rhythms and frequencies are used so ingeniously. Every producer wants to get there.

I produce and then I distribute the music. I never produced music for a label. Also because I would be under an enormous pressure to live up to the expectations.

Minimal music triggers something in a very isolated way. It is ideal for a totally strung-out state of mind in which you do not know anymore who you are, or who your father is.

Jack de Marseille

I don't like to be pigeonholed. I am eclectic. When I started to play in clubs, I noticed that you can get away with a little bit of everything. The djs who really make a difference are those who know how to play a bit of everything, who manage to give a new impulse to their set by playing different tracks. But you have to do it well and you have to specialize. You have to find a balance between key tracks and more difficult things. There's a physical side to our music after all. People have to spend themselves. Everyone has their own definition of music. For certain people, house is dancing. Or the tech house aspect of house. I like the jazzy angle of house, the musicality, the instruments. Intensity is something that I find in techno. I was influenced by electro funk in the 80s, and acid house in the late 80s was a revelation. Vocals don't bother me, if they make me more aware of the music. But I also liked new beat, which had this cool side that you encountered again in techno. Although I studied at the conservatory and know about musical theory, I immediately trust my own ears and instinctively look for sounds, organize, and arrange them. I have to change from time to time and play something else. If I don't do this, I would start to turn in circles. Getting people from different cultures to dance is quite a challenge. It's not an easy thing. You have to observe, you have to nourish yourself with all the emotions you can get from a dance floor. A dj is not a jukebox. He has to guide the dancers and to tell a story at the same time. I look at what I want to play to have an idea. I know the records that are good to start an evening, but I don't prepare my set in advance. I watch and I react. I try to adapt. Every city is influenced by the people who initially created the scene. You have to adapt and still be true to yourself. In Germany, I play techno. In Belgium and Switzerland, it's more funky tech house. In Spain, it's predominantly techno, except in Barcelona and Ibiza where it's house. The more space you have, the bigger the location, the more you need a strong dynamic. People need sound and energy. In more intimate spaces, you can allow yourself to play more mellow and deeper tracks. You can't really do an evening with garage house in a large place, unless you have an extraordinary sound system that plays the music well.

I've always been very stringent and very perfectionist. Now that I've got my own studio in Marseille, I can take my experiments further and do more toying around. I'm not a sound engineer. I proceed by trial and error, but I know what direction I'm going. I usually go into the studio after weekends spent mixing in clubs. I soak up the energy throughout the night. The emotional discharge regenerates me.

S u r geo n

In the early 80s, around the age of 12, I started to play with simple, then current electronic instruments. I had no drum machine, hence it sounded quite experimental. Looking back on it—I still have a stack of tapes at home—it sounds a bit like *musique concrète*, but of course I didn't know about that back then. It's interesting that when you start to make music at an early age, you work without influences. You don't know anything, you just work with the possibilities of the machines, your own ideas, and your own fun. It's an attitude that I still try to have, that I want to regain. This concentration on the situation, on being alone with yourself and the machines. At that time, I was also interested in electro. I liked this artificial, very electronic sound. We were this little circle of friends who exchanged records. For a maxi-single, I had to save my pocket money for three weeks. When hip-hop became increasingly important,

I did not like the egomania of the rappers, and dance music disappeared from my world for a while. Bands like *Coil*, *Throbbing Gristle*, *Suicide*, and *Faust* became important for me. When acid house started, it seemed so naive and basic that I didn't take it seriously at first. It was wasn't exciting enough musically. When I heard the first *Underground Resistance* records I got into it. This was something I could relate to, the industrial aspect. I got more interested in techno when I heard records like the first *LFO* LP and the first *Aphex Twin* releases.

I've always felt that environment and experience have a large influence on my music. I think the main influence Birmingham has had is the fact that if something didn't exist there, we had to make it ourselves. There was no techno club, so we made our own (*House of God*). We'd heard about *Lost* in London, but didn't have the money to come down to London for a night out, so we just made it up as we went along. We had nothing to compare it to. This whole "do-it-yourself" attitude is very strong in Birmingham.

There is now a much bigger network of record distributors, promoters, booking agents, and about one million more djs than when I first became involved. These days I think it's a lot harder to break into the scene than when I first started. Today, people seem a lot more career-minded about trying to break into the scene and working their way up the ladder. The techno scene seems to fold in on itself very easily. Techno influenced by techno, influenced by techno etc.. I don't hear most of the records that are released these days, but that doesn't bother me. I know the good records will find me in the end. Musically, I draw influence from outside the techno scene, whether it's *Coil* or Missy Elliot or *The Velvet Underground*. I try to create my own "blend." Too much techno sounds as if the same producer made it all in the same studio; no character or personality to set it apart from 100 other records. To me, it comes down to the difference between making music and making a product; it depends on the motives behind its creation, but you can always hear them. Electronic dance music is very effective. As long as people want to dance, it will be here. I don't think it will ever be the most popular form of dance music, but I'm sure techno will always be around in some form. I still feel that so much more can be done with techno. There's no point in releasing the same thing again and again. Techno can be anything you want it to be. I think too many people restrict techno by giving it a very narrow set of rules to follow. I like impure techno. Techno is only a part of the music that I like. I don't see myself limited to techno; I am involved with electronic music in general. The shift in the media towards electronic music makes it more popular, more people want to dj than to play the guitar and all that. None of this changes the way I work. The music is the most important thing, there are no real stars anymore

I'm sure most of us remember watching *Dr Who* when we were very young. I used to love the music and sound effects, they were sounds you'd never heard before, not of this world, very dark. My dad had a few Sci-Fi/space themes records by *BBC Radiophonic Workshop*. I really liked these when I was about 4 or 5. Apart from that, I wouldn't say that science fiction is a big influence on me, I don't follow it, but I do draw a lot of influence from external media (Film: Mike Leigh, David Lynch, Francis Coppola; Literature: William S. Burroughs, Bret Easton Ellis; Photography: Cindy Sherman) and other types of music.

Inspiration comes from my life experience and most importantly, my surroundings. I am expressing the feelings of living in a city now. People all over the world living in other cities in decay should be able to identify with these feelings, regardless of their culture, sex, or language. The traditional cultural, lingual, and sexual references have been reduced to a more fundamental and thus powerful level. Hence the album titles *Communication* and *Basic Tonal Vocabulary*. Combined with the power of dance, it's pretty strong stuff. It's not a new idea but I'm trying to refine it.

H ei k o L a ux

Kanzleramt, my label, started in '94, but the bar was around earlier—there was a *Kanzleramt* bar in my old hometown Bad Nauheim. This is where I grew up, and I ran this bar together with my brother, and there was always somebody spinning records. This is the place where Johannes Heil (an artist on *Kanzleramt*) ran into me. He came to this bar and said, "Oh, this is techno, I wanna do this too", and Anthony Rother came as well—I knew him before, but this is how we came together again music-wise. So I actually met all these people there, because I was kind of out there, running a techno bar: everyone who wanted the same music had to check it out. A mutual support developed and it became fertile on a creative level. Only then you start to pursue certain venues and to develop a style.

I never wanted to be pigeonholed. I always wanted to be my own minority, however small. The concept "underground" was developed by people sitting in the basement who just make music for themselves. There's no underground, there's just these loners and their opposite, people who make music for an audience or a market. I would call them craftsmen. In my own tracks, the kick's always the sound. That's what inspires me. I first have to create a sequence and then I add on to it. Otherwise, I won't get far. Normally, nothing remains of the initial ideas behind my tracks. I use them as a springboard for other ideas. I like simple things. I don't know why. I try to combine the maximum of funkiness I can get out of the classic patterns and machines, but from the perspective of, say, a real drummer programming a 909 (drum machine)—I wanted to have it as close as possible to different musicians playing on the same track. I only do music alone, but I do it from the perspective of each different musician. This way I try to bring in a maximum of natural funkiness. Definitely, a little bit of a jazzy influence. On the other hand, it's still techno, I would say maybe breaky techno, because it's music for the floor, and the 4/4 djs can play it because it has the right speed. But it has no 4/4 kick drum, because the 4/4 kick drum has nothing to do with a real drummer. I tend to overemphasize melancholia, which is basically almost kitschy. It 's actually very, very embarrassing to me, but it only becomes kitsch through massive repetition. To me, making music is somehow like striving for a paradise-like state.

The only thing I can reach are people themselves. But they have to meet me half way. As long as they are open for a while and let themselves go, they have the opportunity to feel things the way I intended them to. A club night can be more liberating and more relaxing than a vacation. That's where I start and try to take people on a little trip. The exciting things happen through change. A two-hour straight techno set can't move me anymore. After half an hour, I have to move things in some direction. I like working with vinyl. The imperfections and little problems you have with it force you to improvise. With software something similar probably wouldn't happen. There would be no mishaps. You can shine by overcoming a slip-up. If you manage to handle a set-up that is unstable in many respects, you get a high degree of satisfaction. When you get the right mix as a dj, there's these moments where everything just fits: different sounds encounter each other for the first time and suddenly something happens, no one can explain why, but everyone feels it. That's a technique I also try to use in producing, to celebrate these moments when sequences meet for the first time. It creates an energy that can change the mood in a room.

Language is too imperfect for me. When I want to say something, I can put it in words, but the feeling that someone has who hears the same word is always different. Poets around 1200 still essentially used language to convey their emotional world. I think today things have grown more flat as so many things had to be simplified in our use of language and had to be downsized. Daily soaps, TV trash, they make grandiose things, like "I love you" or "I hate you," sound so trite that in real life you need a five-hour conversation to really set these things straight. Or you have to recourse to massive action to make it clear what you mean. The words at our disposal are always the same and very often they are simply not forceful enough anymore. My music has helped me to balance this. I don't talk, I make music. There's no room for interpretation.

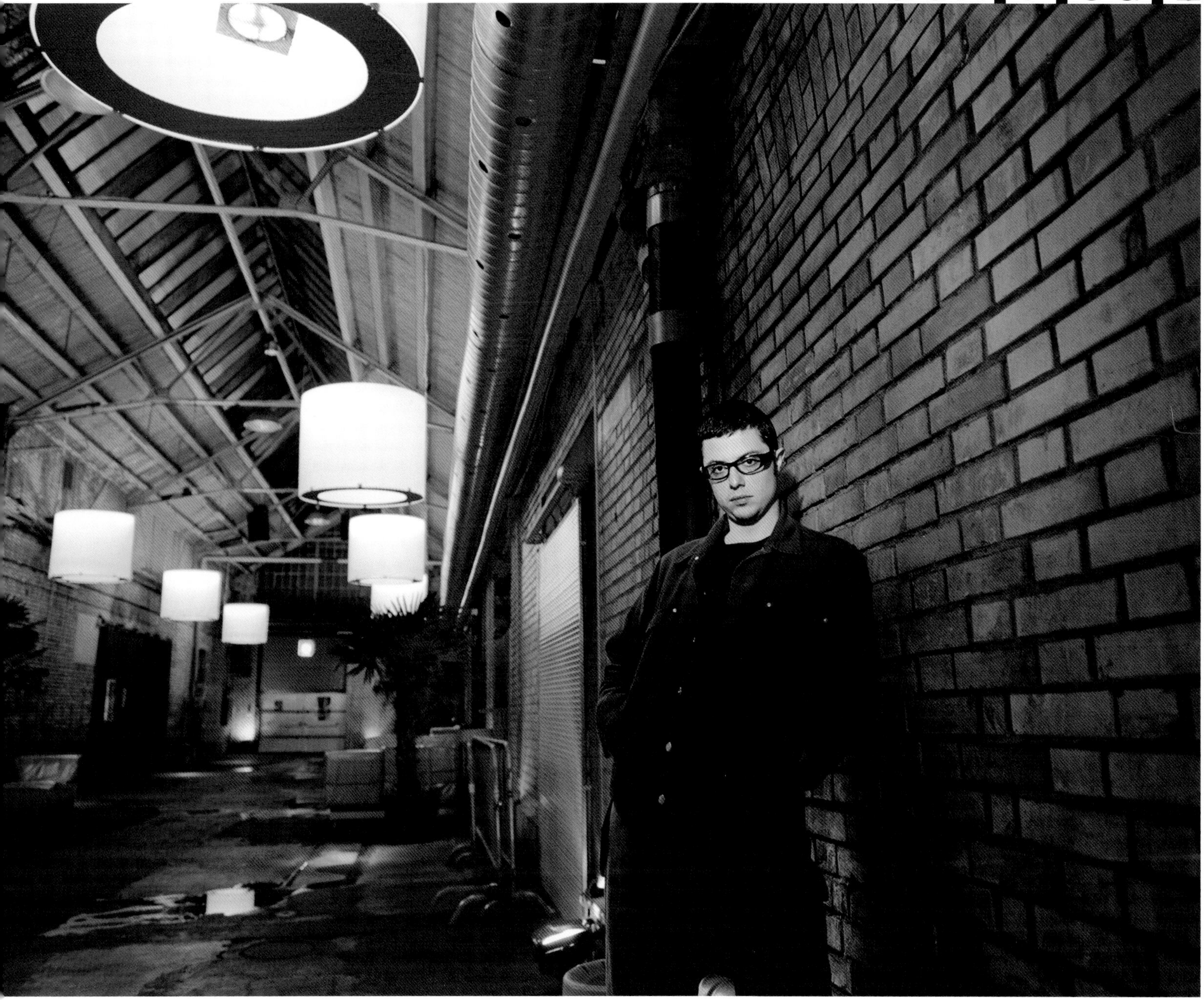

E l ect r ic In digo

Music just came to me. As a child, I was more or less in a passive role, listening to what others played—until I found a top-ten tape that was already a couple of years old. I would endlessly listen to it on an old tape recorder, a kind of a dictating machine . At home, we listened to so-called evergreens (Louis Armstrong, Ella Fitzgerald, Glenn Miller, etc.) and classical music. I learned to play the piano like all Austrian girls do. Later, it was mainly my friends who called my attention to music—around '86, it was East-Coast hip-hop and later, in the late 80s, rare groove—funk and soul of the 60s and 70s, mixed with jazz. At the beginning of the 90s, I more and more got into electronic dance music. DJ Rush on *Saber Records* and *Underground Resistanc*e were decisive for me back then. When I switched from funk and jazz to techno more than ten years ago, I used to explain it like this: To me, techno is the essence of hip-hop, funk, and jazz. Today, this is certainly easier to understand than in the early 90s when techno was considered "German fascist music" in Vienna. I maintain that there is a continuity in my music: a certain funk element and the rather obvious appreciation of the rhythm section in music, drums and bass lines.

I gain from the past, I am into the present, and I believe in the future. Right now there's a strong tendency to revive the past. New wave, punk, EBM: in short, the 80s. I basically like that but I am against the exclusive idealization of the past. I depend on a continuous development, also in regard to myself. I cannot limit this to music alone. The revolutionary thing about techno was less the musical form but its social function, the social structure in which techno took place. Hence, I have to find new social contexts for music—besides continuing to develop new production technologies and techniques. Electronic bass-, respectively rhythm-, oriented music of the last 10, 15 years has shown that it can be communicative and transport feelings and attitudes when played in private spaces. But only in a club or rave context it reveals its full potential, i.e. the intense experience of new social structures. The locations where techno, house, electro, drum 'n' bass are preferably presented can be of a highly different nature: from a cute, plushy atmosphere to austere, dirty industrial halls. What they have in common, however, is that the organizers and finally the visitors more or less cheekily take possession of these locations, alienate them from their original purpose (often in a legal gray zone) and invest them with new meaning. The design of the space, the choice of the location are decisive to the successful creation of a social space. Both the concept of the "club" (meetings on a continuous, regular basis in a particular space), or of the "rave" (the non-recurring, or only occasional, use of preferably unusual locations), in the context of electronic music incorporate the claim to aesthetic avantgardism. An adequate visualization of the (relatively) new character of the music and of the accompanying socially relevant structures induces a process of identification on the part of the audience.

I mainly support my female colleagues, but not just newcomers. I created a web site *http://www.femalepressure.net* featuring a databank of female djs, producers, and visual artists. It's a steadily growing collection of names and addresses that can be searched according to different criteria. Naturally, it's not just beginners, but also many highly professional women active in electronic music. By now, there are around 250 women on *female:pressure*. Today, I am perceived and taken seriously as a dj, not just a female dj. But I always experienced being a woman in this genre as very positive because it was much easier to get a high profile. In the beginning, there were parties that booked me just because I was a female dj, and this would reflect favorably on the promoters. But that never bothered me. Insofar I am for quotas because as long as all of this isn't normal, it has to be pushed a bit.

T o k tok vs. So ffy O

Toktok must always be written in one word. In '93, Toktok was founded in the Trash Chapter of a squat in Berlin Friedrichshain, the *Schizzo Temple*. The activists were Benjamin Weiss as Nerk, Carsten Neubauer as C14, Robert Stadler as Anton Waldt and Fabian Feyerabendt as Fabian Feyerabendt. Stevie as Stefan Küchenmeister (the official *Toktok* dj) joined us shortly afterwards. In the following seven years, nothing special happened, except the founding of our first label *GEMA* with one release of which 500 were pressed and the incredible amount of four sold. That was kind of frustrating at first, but we kept on making tracks, and the editions and sales increased slowly but continuously. We then founded our second label *V-Records*. In '96, we made our first video for C14's track *Sport*, which was shown on *Viva*'s *Berlin House Show* quite frequently . We started to play live in Berlin's cellar clubs for something like 50 Marks (for the then four of us!), organizing our own parties together with people like the brothers Eberhard (aka BassDee & Feed), Tilman (of the legendary *Elektro* club, now owner of Berlin's record shop *RAW*), the *Robotniks* and the incredible *Spiral Tribe* in locations such as old bunkers, the *Elektro*, *Frisör*, *Bunker*, *Sexyland*, or the *Schizzotempel* (now defunct seminal Berlin clubs). With these gigs we didn't really make a fortune, but we had lots of fun (and training), dragging the whole studio to the clubs, plugging it all in, and going for a wild jam that would last up to 24 hours (like our *Krautok* party, for example). A few years later, C14 and Anton Waldt went into musical retirement (C14 started to take his job as a programmer for *Playsta-*

tion games and graphics more seriously, and Anton Waldt concentrated on being a journalist/writer). The rest of us kept on making tracks and releases on *BPitch Control* and played live all over Germany, Austria, France, and finally Spain and Japan. Shortly afterwards, we met Sophia Larsson Ocklind aka Soffy O and decided to make tracks with her. The first track was called *Missy Queen's Gonna Die* and was realeased as a 10" in summer 2000. At the same time, we also started to play live with Soffy O. The track turned out to be a huge club hit, so in spring 2001, *EastWest Records* signed us. A video was shot by Joerg Buttgereit (cult director of splatter/horror movies, like *Nekromantik 1 & 2, Schramm*) whom we have worshipped for his movies since we were kids.

C r i s t i a n Vog e l

Techno is such a strong force and has achieved so many amazing things as a musical form. It questioned and broke down so many barriers in music and the industry, but I would hate to see that wasted. People need to be reminded of how innovative it was, and how it could innovate again. I'm not the only artist doing it, but maybe I'm the only one who's bold enough to stick his neck out and to say that I am trying something different. Obviously, it was initially a teenage drug experience and a rave tape from Coventry. I just remember a sudden understanding of the implications of what was going on. It was like all music had come to an end, and everything had just cracked wide-open, a bit of a cerebral rub down, and it all made sense. I was there and my brain was blown wide open by that music, and thousands of brains were, and it led the way for loads of other people to get into the music industry. It was a fucking revolution. Because I went to college and studied music of the 20th century, I have these ideas about sharing and community and development. The program gave me a firm understanding of that aesthetic, of atonality and texture and various other concepts about music that you might not be able to formulate on your own. But I wasn't propelled into the arty world, as you might expect. In many ways, the program made me certain that I didn't want to go there and make a deeply theoretical, very serious type of music.

I am coming from improvisation. It's very easy to improvise on something that everyone understands. Jazz improvisation succeeded only because it was based on certain riffs people could recognize and perceive as its basis. You always use a certain form in order to manipulate it, but its core remains unchanged. Techno is ideal for this. It's much more fun and it makes much more sense when you come back to something simple while improvising. The beat is something everyone understands; improvising without a beat is very difficult. Not only as a musician, but also as a listener, because the possibilities to find an access to the music are too few. You're always drawn back and forth between two poles: it's either narcissistic, egocentric crap or highly complex, important music. Techno has a basis that is immediately evident, that can be understood with both brain and body. This gives you a great freedom as producer, because you make something that will be understood in any case, yet it can be endlessly expanded. I am always about inventing. I don't use samples. I am the synthesizer type. If there's anything that has influenced my music, it's the machines I work with. I engage with them. I follow them and I want them to follow me. They are the tools I use to express myself, but they are also my partners that I meet with respect. Ever since I was 8 or 9 years old, I have been programming computers. To me, this was always something creative. I was a hacker when I was a kid, member of a gang called *The Powerlords*. We'd hack into systems, nick games, and then spread them around. I did the music on them. My first brush with fame.

I've always made my music with a view that it's got to be played really loud—that's the main thing. When people say it's not club music, it's like, "Well, obviously you've never heard it in a club." Which is understandable, because not a lot of djs are brave enough to stick their necks out and try something different. But I do. My music and the stuff that I mix in dj sets is a lot more mental, but it equally makes you dance. I like to keep a physical energy going. When you play a piano or a keyboard, your hands tend to repeat the same patterns. It's very hard to break away from that. You can use software to disassociate yourself from your own fixed ideas. Introducing random and chaotic elements breaks you out of those moulds and stimulates new ideas. It's essential as far as I'm concerned. Perhaps some of my music can seem a bit serious at times. But I'd like to think it's all counterbalanced by downright stupidity. A big fart noise can do wonders to lift spirits.

I've been on the road every weekend for nearly a decade now , and many times I've found myself pondering the question why I am doing what I'm doing. Usually when I'm hanging around in airports or I'm in a hotel-room bath with the heat lamp on. Over the years the answer changes. When I first started out, it was simply because it was exciting to do what I was doing. Everything was new. It seemed that I was lucky enough to be doing something original. Then there was a need to differentiate my music and myself from the mediocrity that began to saturate the dance-music scene, a mediocrity that was whiting out all the contrasts. This made it really difficult to be original again. Then things became lonely, and I started to do stuff that might bring me back to a community. Then a lot of the good people left the scene, and I found myself doing things to remind newcomers that this music is full of good memories and unique accomplishments, many of which were lost in a tidal wave of gray , brown, and beige stuff. I'm thinking about contrasting the norms, loosening things up. I'm thinking ahead, hoping that by reaching the right ears and putting down interesting reference points, it might cheer some good people up. My messages are changing all the time … I think right now , its about reaching out to dreamers who need reminding that they're not the only ones. My message has some kind of GAFFA attachment that depicts the Sofa Seal of Approval, deadpanning the phrase "I think you're alright. Its OK to have a laugh now."

Chicks on Speed

Even though there are more and more women, there are still too few, but we're glad it's on the way up. During punk, there were a lot of active women on the scene, and now there seems to be a trend that women can relate to and that makes them aspire to what is going on in electronic music.

Alex and I met in art school because we were bored with art school, and I met Kiki, because we both had Japanese boyfriends who spoke Japanese to each other. And then we started to get along better than the boys. Around '94, '95, we used to do this bar called *Maria Bar*, and then Melissa came along one day and had all these slides and really cool things and wanted to show them. We stopped doing *Maria Bar* and then we started doing *Seppi Bar*, a bar for which we used to find different locations and just do a party for a night, maybe once a month or something. Just everything. It wasn't just about music, it was more about just meeting and communication and having fun. And then the music got more important.

We got sort of annoyed with the whole art world and the gallery system and the system of the whole position of the artist and the gallerist and the communication you get with the viewer, and then you don't reach enough people and then that's why we decided to make music

Because it's not so isolated. Or elitist, actually. It's strange, because it gets you away from defining yourself as a fine artist or a musician. So you're kind of floating between that, and then you don't really have this label and it's like, "What you're doing is what you are," this whole identity thing. It's more obscure actually. But not as clearly defined.

It's developed its own sort of direction, its like another facet of the whole thing. It all goes around because we are actually really different, all the three of us, so if someone has one idea, then it gets added to and added to and then it changes and whatever, it's a mish-mash. Visual installations/music and exhibitions are all-important media for us. Recently we have been concentrating on music and the visual content of our live performance. Installations will play more of a role for our group.

We think it's funny how *Macintosh* tells everyone to think differently and use the same computer equipment. As Courtney Love once said about the underground: "A new subculture is born, and within 2 minutes the rights will have been sold to *Nike*."

D J Ru   s h

Be honest. Energy in music mostly comes from being frustrated about not having sex. I do all of it in my music. If I were soft and mellow, I couldn't get rid of it. You are at a party and you are frustrated. You don't want to hear anything that's going to make you feel more frustrated. You wanna leave that behind. So it has to be powerful and in-your-face. It's about being something special. In the beginning, at least. You want to have something to show off. Maybe that has something to do with being gay. Most of what I do is sexual. Gay, straight, whatever. What's that? Gay sex, straight sex? You do something with a man or a woman. It's just sex. I just say what I like, or what I do, or what I would like to do. These are things I am thinking about.

"Club kid" in the US mainly means that you wear what you want. Something unusual. For instance, white make-up and black lipstick and stuff coming up from your hairs and stax that are 20 to 30 centimeters high. That's what we call a "club kid." But I heard that in Europe this means people who do drugs and go to raves. That's different in the States. We call them "rave fuckers." I am not dissing it. It's just what we call them. To each his own.

In Europe, people are more likely to respect you as an artist. Some see you as a star, okay. But most see you as an artist. It's about sharing certain ideas and ideals. In the States, they want to know what equipment I use in order to imitate my sound. And labels cheat the artists. No matter whether it's new labels or old ones. Every time I am in Chicago, someone comes up to me and says that I should come back to make black dollars. What's that supposed to mean? Where's the problem? They just want to fuck with me. I got so tired of being in Chicago, because I felt like I'd done everything, and when I wanted to do something new, everybody would just knock you down and say, "OK, this is not allowed, this is not good, you're stupid for doing this." And then when I went to Germany, it was like I felt free, I can do anything I wanted to do, people don't care. So I just had to leave Chicago. My mother told me, "You know what, you're not happy here no more, just go." The next week I just packed one bag, some records, and went to Germany. I didn't know where I was going but I knew I was going to Berlin—and that's where I went. Of course, it wasn't easy in Berlin in the beginning. But at least it was mysterious. All these ruined buildings. It only became difficult when I had the feeling that I am living here. When the mystery was gone. But nothing keeps me in the USA. Sometimes I think that I have European roots because of the music that I listened to. It was from Italy, Germany, England. I only go to Chicago to visit my family and to produce music.

To be honest, I never really heard Detroit sound until I moved to Berlin, because everyone in Germany was like,"Detroit! Detroit! Detroit!" and that's when I noticed some of the records that were coming out of Detroit. It's funny because a record that I made, someone compared it with Kevin Saunderson, and I couldn't believe it when I heard it. I'm like, "Mmm, it does sound sort of familiar to what he does, like, years ago." So I wouldn't say I was influenced by the Detroit sound, cause I never really knew what they were doing, because in Chicago I was doing disco, stuff like that, so all the newer records and stuff that was made with machines, I wasn't really buying it, so I didn't know what was going on—only the stuff that was made in Chicago, really.

Eastern Germany, Dresden, Cottbus, Dessau: That's where I feel alright. All of sorts of people say, "Come on, look at them." But no one's as good at partying. No one in the world dances like Eastern Germans. The name "Major Rush" comes from djing in Eastern Germany. I was sitting in Chicago and thinking about Eastern Germany. The people there give me so much love when I play. They like what I like: I like it hard. For this I don't want to use the name "DJ Rush." I want something different, something special, something major. Besides, it's something dominant. My other name "Rush 'n' Roulette" is more feminine and it's about dressing up. That's what I always did and always will do. It doesn't mean Rush is gay or Rush is this or that. It's just the way it is. Rush 'n' Roulette talks nasty about his/her feelings, in bed or out of bed. That doesn't mean that Rush 'n' Roulette actually does this, but Rush 'n' Roulette could do this. Rush 'n' Roulette has these fantasies, dreams about it. I can't even say whether this character is a man or a woman.

There's really a story behind my records. The audience has to find the story behind the thing themselves, so I am not telling it. The second thing is that the music is a kind of mirror of how I feel.

D a r r e n P r i c e

Basically, when I started to go out, I immediately discovered acid house. That would've been around the middle of '88 and I started buying records at the same time. '88-'90 were two or three years of constantly going out, clubbing, and taking pills. Towards the end of '89, I bought some decks, although at the time I didn't really plan to be a dj—I was spinning the records in my bedroom for a couple of years, making tapes for myself and my friends. It was my friends who hassled me and told me that I should actually be a dj, and in the end it was Andy Weatherall who got hold of one of my tapes and he gave me one of my first breaks. At the time, he was running a monthly club in Nottingham called *Venus* and he used to get me to warm-up for him; he also recommended me to other people. So it was really him who got me out there djing.

All of the old Detroity kinds of sounds and the nice tunes with strings that they used to make—I used to buy so much of that stuff and it still sounds good now. It hasn't dated like other records have. I mean, the music coming out of Britain at that time was called "progressive house," yet if you listen to those records now they sound awful. More like regressive house! I don't like this attitude where you just let records disappear after a month. They're too important for that. A lot of the old things are simply better. I always liked Chicago acid tracks, but I also like some of the older European stuff, older hard-house stuff. What I do is mixed, but a couple of years ago, when everyone started to play garage and house in London, I opted for the harder side. The energy is decidedly better on techno than on house dance floors. I noticed that again and again. People just get crazier, and I like to move my head really fast. I want to experiment, to do different things. Before, when we didn't yet have enough instruments, we always had to rent a studio, and then you had to hurry because it's so expensive. You can't do what you want. My studio is now right next to Terminal 4's main runway, so we've got the Concorde constantly flying overhead. When these bungalows were built, Terminal 4 didn't exist, but now that it does there are very few families that live around here. It's really very loud. But it also means that the bungalows are very cheap and we can make as much noise as we want.

The Advent

Our music could be described as Martian techno oxy-torched into a galactic bass blast electro whirlpool. Everyone likes to associate us with Detroit, whereas everything we do has nothing to do with Detroit. Detroit is very old techno that's very soulful; we don't do soul, we do very funky tunes. Funky for the mind via the floor. First of all, the groove will lick you, and it might take a while but when you get into the groove, you'll realize it's strong and that you're caught in a trap. Then it'll fuck with your mind. The funk elements in our music appeals to the old and the young, the black and the white. It's there for everyone. *The Advent* stands for electronic funk. The formula itself has always remained the same: dance music with a lot of energy and funk. It's not our thing to let our audience down. We don't want to put off people with a jungle or ambient album. This album-length, forced variety is not our thing. It's about sweaty parties, heavy bass lines, and a dj who plays pumping sound. That's where we're coming from. Remixing gives us the chance to say something different. You know what *The Advent* stands for, but when you get down to someone else's work you can really test the waters and change the formula. You also give those tracks *The Advent* ingredient—you've got to add the juice.

Ever since our fourth EP, we've been touring constantly. I would say that there's very few techno acts that have done this so consequently since the beginning. In the studio, we always have it in the back of our minds that our tracks can adequately be performed live. The live energy has to be the same. In a live set, you can control your music in a totally different way. If the audience really goes for a certain part of a track, you can loop it for 20 minutes. That's why playback shows suck. You can in no way change anything, apart from the fact that it's ridiculous to act as if you were playing a keyboard. It's terribly boring. We're proud that none of our gigs is alike.

There's a note on the back of our first album that says that techno is a global music that cannot or should not be ignored—and now how true that is with the way techno's spreading around the world. You've got Croatia giving the funk, Portugal doing the do, Australia's coming through nicely … There are so many places that are becoming strong outside of the north and that's great. The word "techno" is overdetermined anyhow. There's too many people that associate something totally different with techno than what this is all about. Totally off the point, like the way techno was promoted over the years. Techno is the rock 'n' roll of today in any case.

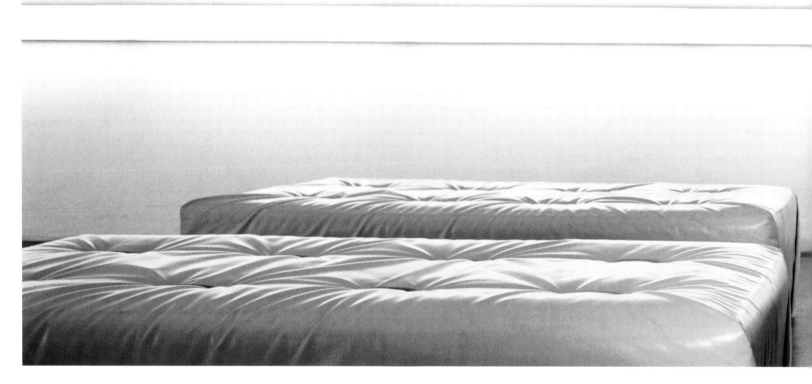

B en   S im   s

I've always listened to groove- or funk-based music, and I would hope my own productions reflect that. Hardgroove, that's what I would call what I play—it's groove-based with a tough edge. If it's been in my box for a few months and I decided to put it out, that's where it goes.

Techno has become a very serious affair. Although I believe in all of these techno ideals, and I prefer to push the development, instead of regressing, but all the same we do tracks that don't take it so seriously. As far as minimalism is concerned, I believe that it sometimes went a bit too far. I am still a dancer and I listen to other djs … It's everything but satisfying to listen to a two-hour set that consists only of brand new records that people don't know. The vibe I care about encompasses classical elements, updated versions of them, breaking down the purist element of it. When I first started playing hip-hop, I was mainly cutting-up records and mixing rap with soul—it was quite jerky. Hip-hop is a lot about power mixing—dropping records with impact. When

I started experimenting with early house/techno, it was much more about beat mixing and finding records that perfectly complimented each other. I basically left behind everything that had anything to do with hip-hop. I wanted to be smooth at any price. No more wild tricks, no more rough cuts. I wanted to create a pleasant flow. Today, I have rediscovered the pleasures of excessive mixing and I try to integrate tricks and techniques from all styles in djing. It's not about playing records, it's about playing with records. I'm first a dj, then a producer. What I'm making is just for me to play with. When I first began buying equipment, it wasn't to start making records, it was to experiment in making music. I only produce in phases and enjoy that. All records are dj tools, if you are a dj. The point I try to make is that my music is meant for manipulation.

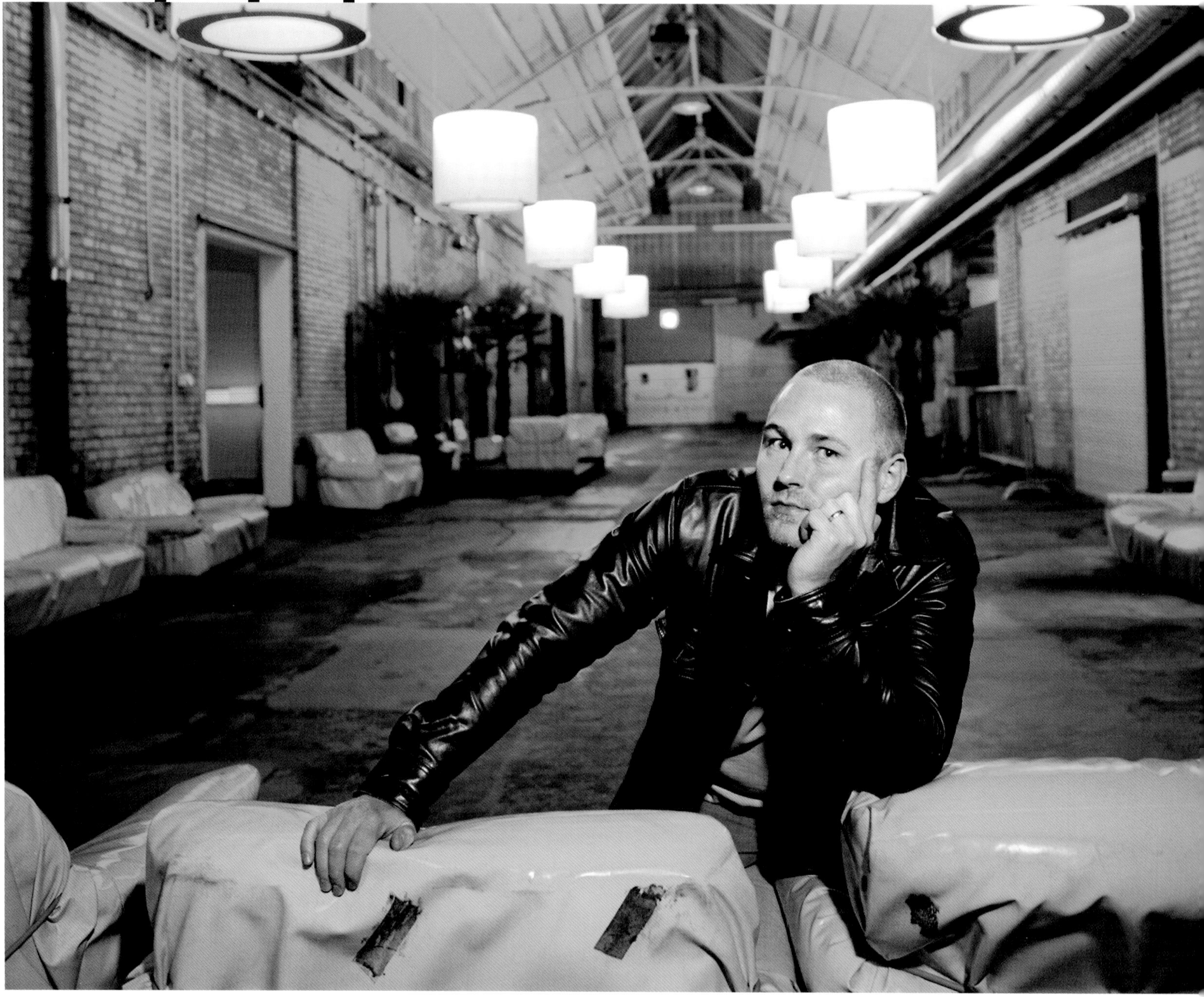

Samuel L. Sessions

People in northern Europe don't want to get into Latin rhythms. They're too cold and they always want it in their face—I don't get it. They only want one type of sound: as monotonous, hard, and fast as possible. For instance, people can't deal with beautifully warm vocal house, embedded in tribal techno. Of course, you're disappointed as a dj when people don't accept something, and you end up reducing your repertoire to what works. I am an entertainer, not a style dictator.

I developed an interest in the organic sounds of the indigenous people of this planet and started to listen to a lot of world music and sample wooden percussion, African chants, samba rhythms, and Latin grooves that would add a certain tribal flavor to the tracks. I try to get women back in the clubs because that's what makes a party work.

Ian Pooley

My mother was always playing records around the house, and I remember that she had two *Kraftwerk* records, which I used to listen to, and then when I was 10, I started buying records myself. I liked house immediately, because I always liked electronic music the best. In the beginning, I was a total *Yello* fanatic. I liked groovy and melodic stuff and pretty soon I got into Detroit. Maybe it was listening to *Kraftwerk* when I was younger that did it. After that, it just developed, I listened to *Inner City* and read *Network Press*. It was just the best feeling to have a *Transmat* record in your hands or a new Kevin Saunderson. As a teenager you really get into this. We painted the *Transmat* logo everywhere. We soon found out what kinds of machines were used by the guys we admired, like those people from Detroit. We found those machines, like the old *Rolands* and old *Yamahas* quite easily, because back in those days no one was interested in them. And when we got them together, we just started. We just did stuff for fun. Me and my mates have always been kind

of independent from the German scene because it used to be very trancey and techno-trancey and we always try to look more over to America, to the scene in America or England and the music coming from there.

House has so many meanings these days, and I think you can do so much more with house than with techno. That's why I stopped buying and playing techno because it's not going anywhere. I always felt that techno needed to be groovier, anyway. I never liked hard techno. If people worked on that aspect more, I'd be happy. There's many different forms of disco house, and I'm not really a fan of the simple, basic disco house tune. Putting one disco loop and a vocal on top is just too simple. OK, you might have a disco sample involved, but you should work with it, not just have a disco sample, but your own instruments, keyboards, and bass line. That's what I think is more interesting. I'm of the opinion that I choose my samples very carefully and I don't use obvious samples. So I was pushed a bit by the record label to give out the samples and next time I won't do that, because I'm quite positive if I don't name those samples, no one will find out. I really don't like the obvious sampled stuff. There is some in it, but I always try to cut it up and make it sound like it's how the original track sounds. About three years ago, I started buying these old 60s records and felt that their tones mixed well with those of house music. There is a good balance to a track when the two styles are combined. It's always a step forward when you mix styles. If you mix house with a bit of indie, you get ambient. If you mix hip-hop with dub, you get trip hop. It's the same thing that I am doing. Of course, you irritate the purists but you'll get used to it.

99

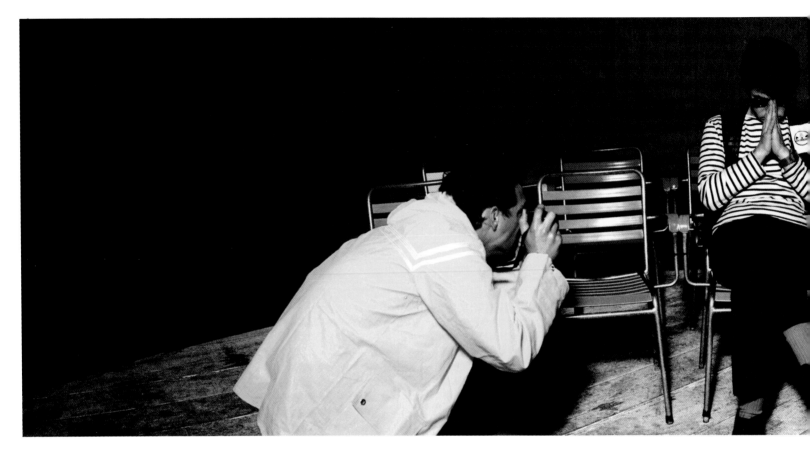

U F O

Art Center College of Design
Library
1700 Lida Street
Pasadena-CA 91103

It's like in fashion. You have *prêt-à-porter* and you have high fashion. And I was looking at the shows and looking at the high fashion in Paris, and I think we work like high fashion or a couturier or a tailor. When it's handmade, it's different than *prêt-à-porter*. People are used to *prêt-à-porter*. Very minimal *prêt-à-porter* like you have in techno, very simple. We maybe try to have a high-fashion style of making music with our limited knowledge. Without being musicians at all, we work with a programmer and we give him directions. It's really like a puzzle that you put together. The big part of it that is important is the recycling of the music. And that way you can get different sounds, old sounds, and give them life again.

A lot of people are not aware about the position of the dj now. The possibilities of the ways that you can use the sample as an instrument. We don't play instruments like a band, but we make an album that sounds as if it were a band. But just we play with tapes and the samples, samples and the sampling machine. When you work with samples, sometimes all the parts come together easily, and sometimes you hear a sound in your head but you can't find the sample that fits. We could use live instruments but that wouldn't be *UFO*, so you end up spending hundreds of dollars on records to find a tiny sound.

We push our limits with each album. We are big thinkers and like big music, and we want to make music that will last forever. So when we get together to make music, nothing is simple. People do such simple things that everyone thinks are so great. It's ridiculous. Minimal music with no melodies is like *Kleenex* music. One track follows the next and follows the next, and none of it stands out.

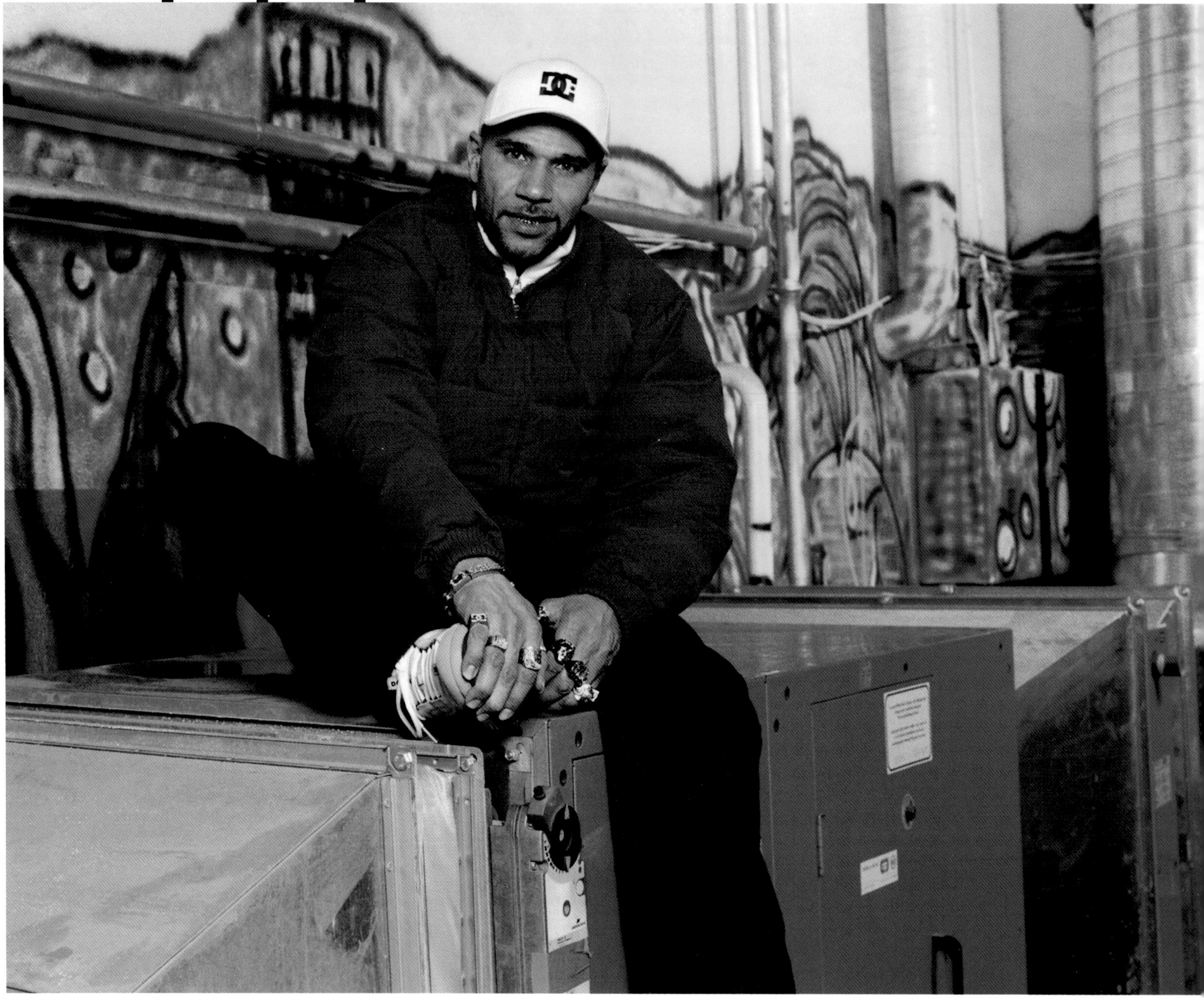

G o l d i e

Some people might call what I do "drum 'n' bass." But I'm not going to narrow it down to what the music industry thinks is commercially viable. I'm not really into narrow thinking. Making this music is like poker. You begin with five cards. You don't play poker with two cards. That's just the rule of the game. Once you have learnt how to play the game, you can bend the rules. I've been in this game for as long as I can remember, seeking out bits of punk, pop, and reggae when I was still a kid in Walsall, London. When the slap-bass days arrived in mid-80s, I started to get into *Loose Ends*, *Change*, and *Maze*, travelling to funk all-dayers. I even gave Rastafarianism a shot, earning myself the nickname "Goldielocks," but then the hip-hop scene blew up and you can't spin on your head if you've got locks. Hip-hop allowed me to express myself artistically for the first time. Doing graffiti art made me learn how to make something out of nothing, and it got me involved in the music scene. I spent time in New York exhibiting my work and appeared in Africa Bambaata's feature film *Bombing* as one of Britain's top graffers. That rocked. In '86, I moved to Miami and started a business selling engraved gold teeth. By '90, I was on the move again to London, where something very special was about to kick off. The club was *Rage* at *Heaven*. Everyone was just going for it. The adrenaline was pumping around the place. I heard djs playing a weird hybrid sound. There was still the late rave stuff, but here was a new sound, a mad fusion of old and new. I'd always been the sort of kid who wanted to belong and now I felt like I'd found a home. In '92 I produced my first track as *Ajax Project*, while I was doing some design and A&R work for the *4Heros*' *Reinforced* label. But at first I was just this deranged kid at Rage with gold teeth shining, this nutter talking a million miles an hour. By late '92, a darker sound was taking over. By '93, recording as *Metalheadz*, I had released my darkcore anthem *Terminator*, lifting the buzz-saw synth riff from Joey Beltram's *Mentasm* alongside the mutating breakbeats that began to characterize darkcore. It was just like rebelling with the music. This darkness was Britain's new urban blues. Dark to me was just a representation of the way people were feeling at the time: there was a recession, and the country was in decline.

The vision I have has been that I'm here to make people have faith. I'm so strong about faith, it's ridiculous. Faith for this huge generation is that it is possible to change everything. And the nature of technology and faith is that science and faith are very, very close. They work parallel, and when you have faith as a barbarian or an artist, you can grasp technology and turn it inside out. You're not supposed to believe in faith, because you can't see it. But I can see money and I can see guns and I can see death, so therefore I believe in that. Fuck this, I have no faith. My whole family has been killed, I'm not supposed to believe anymore. This is the whole job that we have to do in life: to have faith. With music, I wanted to touch it. The tragedy is to get people up to thinking their way to death. They have to build up to that. I'm in a car crash, the crash is happening, it's over before you realize it. We think about death in a very gruesome way, because the way in which we die is horrible and gruesome. I have such an outlook on life now, but I have fears that are built-in because I'm human. Sometimes I have a small fear and when I go out and dj in front of 3000 people, I got butterflies. I always have butterflies, and that's fear, because I don't know what to expect. I never get over this. Every crowd I play, I still have butterflies. The bigger picture is that all I can do as an artist is to provide people with a different way of thinking.

To be quite honest: I'm personal in the music I choose as a dj, because the music is like lots of tiny thoughts and emotions of other people that are part of a bigger picture. I'm just the artist that paints the picture with all of these colours, and the colours are of all these little people that are part of a scene. I'm by no means an ecccentric good dj, I'm more of an artist. No one else could pick those kind of records I get away with , because I'm Goldie and I like weird.

Drum 'n' bass is a way of thinking, it's a world style, it's like graffiti. If a graffiti artist gets a *Macintosh* computer and puts letters into the computer, wraps them around balls, and wraps them around objects, and takes those images, and prints them out and paints them, he's becoming someone that defies and uses technology through his ability to push it. *Macintosh* is in my head for me; my computers are gonna help me bend the music and push it.

L T J B uk em / M C Con ra d

When I was 5 or 6, I started piano lessons, because I used to play around with the piano with one finger and make noises, and my parents thought that was good so they gave me piano lessons. It was Tschaikovsky, Rachmaninov, Beethoven on my parents' part. I quickly developed a hate for classical music, because I wanted to be out there, playing football with my mates, not sitting on a stool playing scales. When I was 10, my piano teacher took me to my first live concert which was Chick Corea at the Royal Albert Hall which sent me into another orbit. He sat there in the Royal Albert Hall with 30 *Rhodes* and *Moog* keyboards and freaked my head out for a year. People like John Barry and Roy Budd really hit me. I was watching those things on TV when I was a kid and that had a massive effect on me. From piano I got into drums and then into trumpet and I was interested in early Mod music like *The Jam*, *The Police*, *The Specials*, and all that kind of thing. I was very attracted to that kind of rock drumming: pcha-boom, pcha-boom, pcha-boom. That kind of thing, which is very drum 'n' bass now anyway. A friend just took me to a soul party, and with my ability to introduce my friends to the music of Chick Corea, Bill Evans, and the early jazz guys and whatever and Dizzy Gillespie. I got into this feeling, this certain vibe. Different people, different times. No one invented drum 'n' bass. These guys invented it a long time ago. We reformulated it and put it out in different ways. The 70s guys, decades ahead of their time. That was it. That was the foundation of my life musically. And for many other people, I think that decade of music was It. And I'm still buying it now. I can't stop. I very quickly built up a massive record collection from the age of 11 or 12. When friends' parties were up, it was like, "Dan's got the music. Come round and play some music, will ya." From that age, I've been behind the decks. Some people who are classically trained haven't got ears or a mind to do things outside that classical training. I'm different because I started having lessons and then dropped it for djing at 15 or 16 and then got into electronic music.

The first time I djed on a turntable was at my friends house in a block of flats called YMCA. And he didn't have *Technics* turntables, he had some other decks with little knobs on them, and I walked into his bedroom and asked, "Hey, what are you doing?" And he's like, "I'm mixing." I thought, "Hmm, well, what are you mixing?" He's like, "Well, it's soul and hip-hop and whatever." This was like in the mid-80s. I thought, "I'll have a go at that," and I started to have a go at it, and that was it. I was at his house every day, mixing. Just mixing. That started a whole load of things. Like going out to warehouse parties, soul dos, *Black Attack*. It was fascinating, because from the twentieth floor of the YMCA I was looking out over the city and I felt like born again. I thought this is something more than what it looks like now. I knew that at the time. I was hooked. Beyond hooked. It was more powerful than any drug.

At the back end of the 80s, I went to a warehouse rave in East London. We were there, in a warehouse with about a thousand people, I remember it like it was yesterday. I remember hearing *Washing Machine* by Mr. Fingers. That tune hit me like the world had ended. I'm in this place where the music's so fucking loud I'm going deaf. I don't know what form of music it is, and it doesn't sound like real music, but it moves me like real music. I thought, "I've got to get into this." That was the first thing I heard and I thought this is so smooth with so much feeling, and makes my hair stand on end, and yet it's not real music. And that was the start of my wanting to find out about electronica.

My success has been luck but it's also been graft. I've given up my whole life. I don't have a life. Unfortunately, that's what you've got to do. Then again, you might do that and not get anywhere. I've been very, very lucky. I get up in the morning, go to bed at 4 or 5 in the morning. I do the same things 7 days a week and it's all to do with this place. I don't go out at weekends. I don't go out for drinks with my mates, I don't have a life.

I think music is something that can take you by surprise you and make you feel a certain way anytime. You can't compare crowds because people get into music in so many different ways. You might get a noisy crowd, but a quieter crowd might be more appreciative than a noisy crowd. You don't know how someone's feeling inside his or her mind. They don't have to be jumping up with their hands in the air to express it. You kind of know when you connect with an audience on a musical level, whether it be a mad or quiet audience.

Jum pin ' J ac k F ro st

I've always been into diverse things. I used to be in a famous dub sound system in Brixton called *Frontline International*. At the height of my days in that environment, I just got bored and thought, "I need a change." That's when I started to go to places like the *Africa Center* and met people like Mad Hatter Trevor and Jazzie B. That really heavily influenced me as I got into the funk thing. Even though the music seems to have developed and things have changed a lot, I've always been the same. I've always been into funky, hard stuff, but I think the older I get, the jazz is coming out a bit more. I'm really into jazzy stuff now. It's just been a natural progression from year to year, from vibe to vibe really. There's a group of people that adapt to change, and another group that set the change. I think I've always been in the group that has set the change. We thought, "Fuck it, we've had enough of this now, or we're getting bored of this now, we're going to move on." That's just the way that it has always been. Love it or hate it, it's up to you. Take it or leave it, that's the way I'm looking at it. Right now, I want some George Clinton 21st-century cyberfunk business and we're going to recreate that vibe again.

I've had people standing there, looking at me with their arms folded like, "What is this?" When I first played tracks like *It's Jazzy* and *Brown Paper Bag*, the whole rave was looking at me like, "What are you on?" I'll always be like that, I'll always be the man you come and hear and think, "What happened?" It's good for the scene, because otherwise it's just going to stand still and no one is going to take chances, then what are we going to do? Input from everyone makes the scene, instead of everyone bashing out the same tunes or on a similar vibe. If everyone does their own thing, then you get a real wide range of music. Not everyone comes from the same background and not everyone is influenced by the same things, so obviously not everyone's music is going to be the same. London is the most cosmopolitan city in the world and this music is a reflection of that.

If you got to know me, you'd think to yourself, "This guy doesn't even seem like a dj." You come to my house and there's nothing to indicate what I do, only in one room. I don't live in that world; my friends aren't interested in it, so there's no "Yeah, Jack" and pats on the back. There's no pats on the back for me, I do what I do and that's it. When people start dealing with me like that, I feel a bit uncomfortable with it. That's why it's sometimes hard for people in my position to find new girlfriends, for example. Just take me as me, how I am, because at the end of the day I'm no star or anything, I'm just a dj, that's all. I think that because I don't let a lot of people into my world, I'm not immediately approachable. I'm not that kind of guy I just prefer to do my job. I've gotten better, though, because I've had to learn to deal with it. Before I was like, "Listen, I don't want to know, I just want to play my records, don't talk to me, just leave me alone." All the attention was hard for me to deal with. People want to come up to you and talk to you, and it's nice, I love it, but sometimes people don't understand that you might have talked to 100 people already that night and they want to talk to you for half an hour as well. It can get a bit much.

J.   Majik

I was about 14. It was really just enthusiasm. I suppose if I'd grown up ten years earlier, everyone would have wanted to be a footballer. In my generation, the whole acid house thing was just starting when I was 13 or 14. A lot of my friends were quite a bit older than me and the cool thing to do was to try to be a dj. We used to go round to each others houses after school and rather than kick a ball about the garden, we'd all mix and compare what new tunes and what new white labels we'd got our hands on. It was almost kind of infringed on me as a kid and then I was lucky enough to meet a few people that had connections with promoters and people in clubs and I got a few warm-up sets. I think a lot of it is who you know when you're first starting out and getting that foot in the door. The first track I made was called *6 Million Ways To Die* with Lemon D which went on Lemon D's label. About a couple of months after that, I met Goldie, and at the time he was scouting for *Reinforced* and looking for new music and stuff, and he kind of took me under his wing. I played him all my stuff that was half-finished, and he was kind of leading me in the right direction and helped me out with sounds and stuff. He was like a real a mentor to me; after all, I was growing up and I was still 14 or 15. Goldie gave me the confidence to make the sort of music I wanted to make which was really what I'm making now. It wasn't accepted back then, it was too experimental. I think one of the better decisions I've made in the past was not signing up to an album deal with the majors back in '96. It didn't feel right at the time and I think that a lot of drum 'n' bass artists weren't expecting the sort of pressure they were put under, with very few having come out of the whole experienced unscathed. The key for me is to build my own thing up and though it may take years of releasing records on my own label, I'm free to concentrate on the music and be able to look at the long-term picture, while not giving anything of myself away to someone else.

I'm just so slow in the studio, and it takes me quite a while. I need to listen to things, and have a bath and have it on in the background, and listen to it in the car. Just kind of live with the tune for a bit, and not just getting a loop going and mixing it down. A lot of the time, I put the loop away, and leave it to kind of ferment in the computer and then maybe come back to it a couple of months later. You come back to it with a fresh angle. To me, the vocal edge gives it a bit more: you can walk out of a club and actually remember a tune. It makes drum n' bass more memorable, rather than just hearing acid basslines and fucked-up sounds. I think it does make it more accessible to the average Joe Public, but at the same time it's still underground, still really club, and really in the right place. That's the thing, just getting big tunes that are still underground but could cross over without selling out, that's what its about to me. I think there's too much music around at the moment which is just noise to me. You can go to a club and everything sounds the same, everything you hear has that two step and industrial noises. What I'm trying to do is move away from that, still maintaining the hard beats and analogue kind of sounds but bringing some music into it, to create more of a groove. I've found that if you go to America and just play noise without any melody or hook, its really non-descript for them and they don't know what's going on. If there's some music in there though it gives them something to relate to. People should remember that it isn't their underground thing and they haven't had the last eight years of what we've gone through in the UK—they want something they can groove to. I've never understood the mentality of people who want to "keep it underground." Would they rather sell a couple of hundred records or make music so dark that nobody else liked it? The scene has damaged itself in its preciousness, holding back some tracks on the dub-plate circuit for months at a time, just a single example. With such a large proportion of people hearing the records through dj sets or resources like *Napster*, an already short shelf life is only getting shorter and I feel the best thing for this music to proceed is to get the records out as quickly as possible.

D J   H yp e

I was caught by the first wave of break dancing in Europe, like many of my generation. But I only started to seriously write in '87. In '88 I got my first turntables and my first mixer (without cross fader). Then it slowly built up. I was oriented towards scratching and producing right from the beginning. I only learned how to properly mix in the early 90s.

Hip hop didn't come from nowhere. There were influences from funk, jazz, reggae, but also German rock productions like *Niagara*, *Can*, or even Hildegard Knef. I like stuff by the Average White Band just as much as James Brown, Bob James, or Herbie Hancock.

E d R u sh

Originally, I started out making tunes when I was about 15, in my bedroom. Back then, we were bang into all the ravey stuff. Hardcore and techno. Before, I was into electro and hip-hop, then I went to some mad *Spiral Tribe* job in Oxford. That was the switcher. That was it for me. I started living on the road with a bunch of travellers and they did their own sound system and organized parties.

The music we make is not particularly from the hip-hop corner, it's from the future. It's about pushing things to extremes. Not just having a big, loud, heavy bass, but having it big, loud, heavy, and so distorted it totally fucks you up. I'm basically into this eerie, futuristic *Blade Runner*-ish feel. People like to put you in pigeonholes, but I must admit that of all the sounds I hear in the studio when I'm making a track, the one that drives me the most is a hard sound. Sound with attitude in it. The dark sound really gets my blood going. My heart is in hard, industrial records. I mean, the world's a damned place. It somehow reflects how people feel. Surving a nuclear explosion and then dying from the fallout, that's a dark thought. We're destroying the planet, the next generation will not have much to laugh about. Driving around in this fucking van all day long drives me crazy. Damn traffic, so when I get to the studio, I'm in a bad mood and I want to hear heavily distorted beats, tough amen breaks.

A lot of people didn't think the dark scene was going to last, but it keeps pushing its head above the water. Dark tracks keep coming round and blowing everyone away. The production in dark tracks is very advanced. There's a much better use of technology. The sounds are more twisted, because there's no need for a clean production like in more jazzy tracks. People want to push everything to max. However, we also use quite a lot of strings and little sounds that sound good when they bounce off each other. We're just trying to get a wider soundscape, layered tracks, and that involves using strings. It's quite nice to mix a nice *Rhodes* chord with dark riffs, the contrast works. We're just experimenting. Some days we're doing things, I wouldn't say light, but the vibe isn't so grim! Always trying to do something different has been the main thing that has powered me. Once you've found a formula that works, be it the beats or the way that you arrange a track, it's very easy to just stick to it. That's boring. It's nice to try and really push the boat out. I've never intentionally wanted to do something that will change everything. We just try and do things that sound different and are interesting to listen to, yet still work on the floor.

Mikky B.　　　　　**Deetron**　　　　　**Bang Goes**

Resident DJs

Gangsta

Styro 2000

Eric Borgo

Art Center College of Design
Library
1700 Lida Street
Pasadena-CA 91103

Special thanks to all those who made this adventure happen from the very first hour and for all those who support our present and future ideas:

Aeberhard Robert Abegg Blagoje Abegg Ljubinka Aeberli Michi Aicher Adi Allenbach Andreas Allenbach Christian Ambrosio Maja Amstutz Marlyse Andjelkovic Danijela Aregger Karin Bader Peter Beer Urs Betschart Irene Bilat Sophie Billeter Vanessa Bischof Werner Bischofsberger Thomas Boner Joerg Boppart Tanja Bösch Urs Braegger Matthias Breitschmid Christian Bruederli Martin Brurderlin Andrin Brusa Thomas Bucher André Buschor Fabiola Calabrese Claudio Carish Andrea Cerddor Adrian Cicco Daniele Cretanovic Dragon Cucuzza Marco Cvstanovic Jovan Dahinden Olivia Dauwalder Hans Davatz Christian Dayen Annik De Haan Martina Deetron Deuber Christian Deutsch Gabriela Dietiker Michi Dold Heiko Donni Alessandra Purgnat Claudia Egli Anja Egloff Michael Ehrat Adrian Eichholzer HP Esslinger Fabian Estermann Josef Estermann Robert Fehlmann Jeffrey Felix Peter Figlestahler Peter Filisetti Sarah Franke Peter Fray Simon Frei Marianne Friedrich M. Frigg Martin Galamb Annido Gehrig Reto Gehring Caroline Gétaz Edouard Godet Midi Göllner Wolfgang Graeub Nick Graf Andreas Gregorio Toni Gugg Bruno Haemmerli Thomas Hari Alexandra Hawle Michael Hegnauer Ch. Heitzer Alexandra Hauri Ernst Hildebrandt HG Hiltl Rolf Hinnen Bruno Hirschi Beatrice Holy Mischa Huber Bruno Huber Erwin Huebscher Martin Huegli Julia Huegli Peter Imfeld Mike Isler Jakob Itschner Monika Jaberg Renate Jeabsakaran Siva Jeanguenin Arthur Jellici Johanna Jesco Schuck Jiri Rainer Jochum Emanuela Jordi Hanspeter Jouffroy Aurora Kaiser Stefan Kaufmann Peter Kaufmann Pierre Keller Walter Kistler Patricia König Dani Kramer Christian Kuhn Rainer Kummer Martin Kutner Gabi Küttel Beat Landolt Konrad Lanz Danielle Ledergerber Elmar Leuthold Felix Levis M. Claire Locher Adalbert Lüthi Daniel Määtämen Kirsti Makosch Ben Martelli Kathrin Marti Doris Martinez Carmen Maurer Esther Meier Marcel Meier Mario Meier Marion Meier Martin Meier Peter Meier Philipp Meier Ruedi Mensing Chris Menzi Renate Mettler Tanja Meyer Arnold Meyer Daniel Meyer Gretchen Minus 8 Mr. Mike Muenger Irene Muff Bruno Müller Roger Natascha Mouzo Netsch Carla Nobs Claude Ott Daniel Ott Maria Paolo Fedrigoli Pellanda Nava Perez Dasha Petignat Alain Pradal Ariana Praz Stéphane Reinhart Andreas Reymond François Rickenbach Suso Riesen Patrick Ritz Nadja Rothenberger Andrea Rothenberger Flurina Ruf Markus Rutkowsky Niklaus Schaad Stefan Schaer Roger Schaffer Urs Schmid Eduard Schmid Reto Schönenberg Werner Schopferer Gisela Schuller Nicole Setter Tamara Short Dominic Sieber Nadine Sobrado Nicole Spleiss Christian Stauffer Urs Sydler Frank Tabatà Tabs Fabian Tavarez Franmil Tavarez Jorge Tellenbach Markus Thar Evelyn Thavarajah Waran Thoeni Corinne Tigges Charles Todesco Roland Tonetto Daniel Tschopp Sybil Ujfalsui Svetlana Ullrich Markus Urech Eva Vaccaro Marina Vazques Fanny Vogel Hans Georg Von Gunten Reto Wallner Sandra Waser Silvio Weber Sabine Weilenmann Jules Weiss Tamara Wichser Hans Wiesmer Susanne Wildhaber Notker Wyss Britta Zambonin Markus Zbinden Roland Zehnder Joerg Zimmermann Rolf Zinniker Christina Zuzak Guggi

Art Center College of Design
Library
1700 Lida Street
Pasadena-CA 91103

Walter Huegli (ed.) in collaboration with Martin Jaeggi
Raw Music Material / Electronic Music DJs today

Design: Steidl Design, Steidl with Claas Möller

Color separations: Steidl, Göttingen

Printing and production: Steidl, Göttingen

Binding: Buchwerk Darmstadt

© 2002 for the photographs: Arsène Saheurs, Zürich

© 2002 for the texts: Masani's Ambient Media, Zürich

© 2002 for this edition: Scalo Zurich—Berlin—New York

© 2002 for the music: the copyright owners as listed in the tracklisting

Head Office: Weinbergstrasse 22a, CH-8001 Zürich, Switzerland

Phone: +41 1 261 09 10, fax: +41 1 261 92 62

e-mail: publishers@scalo.com, website: www.scalo.com

Distributed in North America by DAP, New York City,

in Europe, Africa, and Asia by Thames and Hudson, London,

in Germany, Austria, and Switzerland by Scalo.

All rights reserved. No part of this book or the enclosed music CDs may be reproduced in any form

by any electronic and mechnical means (including photocopying, recording, or information storage and retrieval)

without the prior written permission of the publisher or the respective copyright owner.

First Scalo Edition 2002

ISBN 3-908247-51-9

Printed in Germany

Art Center College of Design
Library
1700 Lida Street
Pasadena-CA 91103

Dave Angel Track 1 Endless Motion (Dave Angel / courtesy © R & S Records)

Misstress Barbara Track 2 Effect Karma (Misstress Barbara / courtesy © Relentlessmusic)

Pascal F. E. O. S. Track 3 I Can Feel That (Pascal F. E. O. S. / courtesy © ICM/Hanseatic)

Ricardo Villalobos Track 4 Arise (Ricardo Villalobos / unreleased, courtesy © Ricardo Villalobos)

Jack de Marseille Track 5 Bump (Jack de Marseille / courtesy © Wicked Music)

Surgeon Track 6 Ice (Anthony Child / courtesy © Tresor)

Heiko Laux Track 7 Kick and Kiss (Heiko Laux / Kanzleramt Music)

Electric Indigo Track 8 Comin' At You (Electric Indigo & Dani D. Caretta / courtesy © Pornflake Records)

Cristian Vogel Track 9 Esquina Del Sol (Cristian Vogel / courtesy © NovaMute/Original Artists)

Chicks on Speed Track 10 Glamour Girl (Christopher Just/Logan Moorse Murray-Leslie / Chicks on Speed Recor

Darren Price Track 11 4 S.E.M' Are Cooking (Darren Price / unreleased, courtesy © Darren Price)

The Advent Track 12 Ice Planet (Cisco Ferreira / courtesy © Kombination Research/Planet Phuture)

Ben Sims Track 13 Remanipulator (Ben Sims / courtesy © Primate Recordings)

Samuel L. Sessions Track 14 Velvet (Samuel L. Sessions / courtesy © SLS)

Ian Pooley Track 15 Balmes (Ian Pooley / courtesy © V2 Records GmbH)

DJ Hype feat MC Fats Track 16 Peace and Love (Kevin Ford / courtesy © True Playaz Music)

LTJ Bukem Track 17 Rainfall (D. Williamson / courtesy © Good Looking Music/Warner Chappell Music Ltd.)

Motion Track 18 Remedy (Motion & Hanna Collins / courtesy © Infrared Music)

Art Center College of Design
Library
1700 Lida Street
Pasadena-CA 91103